LUCK
A Secular Faith

LUCK
A Secular Faith

WAYNE E. OATES

Westminster John Knox Press
Louisville, Kentucky

Book design by Drew Stevens
Cover design by Tanya R. Hahn

First edition

Published by Westminster John Knox Press
Louisville, Kentucky

This book is printed on acid-free paper that meets the American National Standards Institute Z39.48 standard.⊗

PRINTED IN THE UNITED STATES OF AMERICA

95 96 97 98 99 00 01 02 03 04 — 10 9 8 7 6 5 4 3 2 1

Library of Congress Cataloging-in-Publication Data

Oates, Wayne Edward, date.
  Luck : a secular faith / Wayne E. Oates. — 1st ed.
    p.   cm.
  Includes bibliographical references.
  ISBN 0-664-25536-1 (alk. paper)
  1. Providence and government of God. 2. Fate and fatalism—Religious aspects—Christianity. I. Title.
BT135.O28 1995
231'.5—dc20   94-19996

To Roy Lee Honeycutt, Ph.D.
President Emeritus
The Southern Baptist Theological Seminary

Contents

Acknowledgments

I am indebted to President Roy Lee Honeycutt and the faculty and staff of the Southern Baptist Theological Seminary for the environment of learning and enquiry they provided for me to produce this book. Especially helpful have been the staff of the Office Services and the work of Keitha Brasler in her preparation of the first draft of the manuscript. I am indebted also to Becky Timerding for the preparation of the final draft of the book. Without their competent help I could not have done this work.

I appreciate also the fellowship of the other two senior research professors at the seminary, Professors Henlee Barnette and Samuel Southard. Several sections of this book were lively topics of conversation among the three of us.

Acknowledgment of material taken from other sources is listed in the notes at the end of the book, but double acknowledgment of appreciation is expressed here.

Preface

S ometimes the automatic thoughts that leap into a person's consciousness, thoughts that he or she blurts out without premeditation, reveal more about one's true belief system than carefully thought-out statements. For example, on one occasion, a man said to me: "I have always been very *lucky* at praying." At another time, the nurses at a hospital called me to see a patient on their floor. They said that he was to have heart bypass surgery the next day and was extremely anxious. When I went to his bedside, he was indeed in a severe panic reaction. He said: "I'm scared to death! It's what these nurses said. They told me that the surgeon who is going to work on me has operated on over a thousand other patients and all of them lived and have done well. Now, Reverend, you know that nobody is perfect. He's got to lose sometime, and I'm going to be the time he loses!"

He felt that the odds were against him and that he was a "marked man." It took me some time to bring calm and relaxation to him and to shift his attention away from the "odds" to the reality that he was not in just the surgeon's hands. I encouraged him to place his life in the loving care of the God of our Lord Jesus Christ. We prayed for his surgeon, his family, and his own "calm and heavenly frame," to quote William Cowper's hymn "O for a Closer Walk with God." I was trying to counterpose a belief in God's loving care and providence over against his anxiety-ridden belief in the odds that were—according to him—against him in a world of good luck/bad luck.

The more one listens for these impulsive utterances, the more one discovers that many people are guided more by their trust in good or bad luck than by the conviction that their lives are in the hands of God. The opposite of this belief in luck, the odds, and chance is faith like that affirmed by Shadrach, Meshach, and Abednego in their response to Nebuchadnezzar's threat to put them in the fiery furnace if they did not bow down and worship his pagan god. They said: "If our God whom we serve is able to deliver us from the furnace of blazing fire and out of your hand, O king, let him deliver us. But if not, be it known to you, O king, that we will not serve your gods and we will not worship the golden statue that you have set up" (Dan. 3:17–18).

The dramatic difference between such an affirmation of faith in God and "trusting in luck" or "mistrusting luck" underlines my assumption that luck is a secular faith. Many worship luck, fate, fortune, chance, or the odds. This blind allegiance to luck probably has ancient origins that perdure until this day like a sort of petrified forest of ancient animistic religious practices, remnants of occult taboos, and the warding off of evil spirits and the invitation of friendly spirits. These practices continue in contemporary life right alongside Christian worship, as do the winter solstice rituals of Santa Claus and *Tannenbaum* trees at Christmas or Easter eggs and rabbits at Easter. Yet the tacit worship of luck, prevalent as we will find that it is, goes unnoticed, unexamined, and taken for granted. The Greek philosopher Socrates said that "the unexamined life is not worth living."[1] Therefore, the purpose of this book is to examine the pervasive belief in luck and assess its prevalence, lest we continue to take it for granted and let it go unexamined. This secular faith will be contrasted with belief in the providence of God in Jesus Christ. Further, the ways in which pious religious utterances mask a good luck/bad luck belief will be identified.

The worship of luck is not new. Roman theology bears witness to the long history of the worship of luck. (Is it not interesting that we think of Roman and Greek belief in their pantheon of gods as "mythology" when in fact it was their theology?) Servius Tullius, a legendary king of ancient Rome, was reputed to be the founder of the cult of Fortuna, the goddess of fortune or luck. Fortuna had two forms: Fortuna Muliebri, the goddess of womanhood, and Fortuna Virilis, the goddess of manhood. Fortuna Primigenia was the firstborn of Jupiter. Her wisdom was mediated through divination, and an oracle was built to her honor. Her cult was brought to Rome during the struggle with Hannibal. Altars were raised, such as those to Good Fortune, Bad Fortune, and Private Fortune.

This worship tapped into the awareness of the fortuitous elements in human experience. In Latin, *forte* means "by chance, accidentally, or as it happens." Fortuitous in English refers to that which just happens or is produced by fortune or chance. As early as 1711, Joseph Addison, in *The Spectator,* said: "The highest degree of Wisdom Man can possess is by no means equal to fortuitous Events."[2] Fortuitous events, chance, luck, it seems, had at least a demigod status in the belief systems of the English-speaking world.

The worship of Fortuna in Rome involved a cult of worshipers. The very nature of the belief in luck or fortune tends to generate cultic groups of people, even though many devotees of luck live lonely, isolated lives. Luck has many cults in American life today. Devotees are fervent in their pursuit of cultic rituals and the investment of their hopes, money, and time in the practices of these cults.

For example, I have before me an advertisement of the First Church of the Ark of Light, which is located in a nearby town. It is a "non-profit, nondenominational organization." On its roster of leaders are eleven different practitioners, some of whom practice tarot (the interpretation of fortune with playing cards), three crystal ball readers, one star or astronomical interpreter, one interpreter of the mysteries of the alphabet, and several other interpreters of fortune or good and bad luck. That astrology is alive and well in America was seen in the widely publicized consultation of astrologers by Nancy and Ronald Reagan.

This book has two parts. The first part, "Belief in Luck as a Way of Life," has six chapters. They are essentially philosophical-theological essays about the various forms that luck takes in our society, contrasted with the affirmations of the Christian faith. The second part, "Responses to Luck by Pastors and Churches," is devoted to pastoral and church responses to the secular faith of luck. Chapter 7 comes to grips with what to think and do as pastors, chaplains, and pastoral counselors about the clinical appearances of the "horizontal religion" of luck: that is, a secular belief that omits the vertical belief in God as we know God in Jesus Christ. Chapter 8 suggests ways congregations can respond to luck, chance, probability, and even gambling as the church ministers to families, makes decisions, and does its work in the community.

Part 1

Belief in Luck
as a Way of Life

1. Luck or Providence?

*E*ach of us comes into the world with a set of givens, unavoidable and unchangeable conditions over which we have no control and to which we must respond. With very little reflection we can identify several such givens. Our birth itself is a given over which we have no control, as is the place where we are born. We have no control over whether we are born into a poverty-level ghetto existence or into an affluent family and community; we can only respond. Furthermore, embedded in the place of our birth is the given of a social caste or class into which we are born. If we are born into a caste, we are locked-in to the living conditions, kinds of work, the availability of education, and other aspects of the group to which our parents belong. However, if that social group is a class, it is likely that social customs, schools, churches, and other social institutions permit and even encourage and facilitate our movement out of that class into a better situation in life. Or we can choose to capitulate to our given station in life and seek fulfillment within it.

As we continue to live and grow, we enter by choice or necessity into other givens. The best example is that of becoming a parent. When a child is born to us, nothing in time or eternity can change the fact that we are parents of that child. He or she will always be our child, and we will always be his or her parents.

In our particular era, when gender, race, and sexual orientation are issues of intense concern, we can recognize these factors as the givens of a person. An individual may be a woman or man, a person of a particular race, a person of homosexual or heterosexual orientation; or the individual may combine two or more of these characteristics. These are givens of one's common lot in life.

Persons can accept these conditions and view their place in life to which they have been assigned as bad luck. Or they can protest and lobby for their human rights before the law, such as their rights of employment and freedom from harassment. Or they may demand that they be recognized as children of God just as they are.

Another given in life is our age. Jesus asked, "And can any of you by worrying add a single hour to your span of life?" (Matt. 6:27). The date of our birth, and consequently our age at any given time, is one of the "moving immovables," or givens, of life. The responses we make to our age once again call for a particular attitude, frame of meaning, or interpretation by which we live.

Each one of us has both a genetic uniqueness and the power to make our own personal decisions in response to the given situations of our life. We can be either proactive or reactive in responding. The lifestyle that we choose can enable us to develop our own personhood out of our genetic heritage and the sociocultural situations we face.

The final given of life is death itself. Death sooner or later does not take no for an answer. We die in different ways, but everybody dies in some way—by accident, illness, suicide, homicide. Faith in Jesus Christ looks death straight in the face and does not blink. Apart from the faith in Christ, a person tends to think that he or she will never die. Jonathan Swift, in his *Gulliver's Travels,* describes the "Struldbrugs," persons born into the world with a "red, circular spot on the forehead . . . which was an infallible mark that it should never die." By the time they came to eighty years of age they became "opinionated, peevish, morose, vain, talkative, but incapable of friendship and dead to all natural affection. . . . And whenever they see a funeral, they lament and repine that others have gone to a harbor of rest, to which they themselves can never hope to arrive."

Nevertheless, the Struldbrugs' bodies continued to suffer the same as those of other persons. The difference was that other people could die and they could not. Death was a privilege denied them! Swift's angle of vision shows the imaginative outcome if the belief that we would never die were really so.[1]

What are our options in dealing with these and the other givens of life?

SACRED OR SECULAR OPTIONS

The sacred option for dealing with the givens of life springs from a steadfast faith in the providence of God. This choice is perhaps less taken today because we are living in an era in which the providence of God is not generally recognized or considered. As William G. Pollard, an executive director of the Oak Ridge Institute of Nuclear Studies, says:

Among the key elements of the historic Christian faith which are difficult for the modern mind, there is none so remote from contemporary thought forms as the notion of providence. The central Judeo-Christian apprehension of events in individual life and in history . . . has lost all meaningful context.[2]

Thus a believer in providence, although not able to see the hand of God at work in a given situation of one's lot in life, nevertheless holds to the faith that God will deliver him or her from that forced situation according to the distinct purpose God has for his or her life. Therefore, the believer can put up with the oppression of the givens of the present moments of life, live by faith not knowing where he or she is going, but look forward, as Abraham did, "to the city that has foundations, whose architect and builder is God" (Heb. 11:10).

This faith in providence is lived in a community of faith, not in isolation and self-sufficiency. People in this community bear the burden of their common lot in a fellowship of suffering.

The other option, the secular option, for dealing with the givens in life is to believe in luck. This faith looks upon the givens, as we will see in subsequent chapters, as a game of chance. The probabilities can be mathematically figured. The chances, or odds, can be bet upon, and even life itself can be risked "on a bet." Whether one wins or loses is determined by fate.

This approach is a self-sufficient faith that trusts that one's own skill at calculating the odds will enable one to triumph over whatever happens. As we will see, often this faith is a lonely, impersonal faith. Yet it has a tenacity that often exists as a subsoil beneath superficial religious faith. Hence it must be taken seriously and understood in more than a humorous or flippant way.

In posing the belief in luck as a secular faith, I am taking the word *secular* to mean that which pertains to the worldly or temporal as distinguished from the spiritual or eternal. It refers to a particular generation of humankind and not to the everlasting realities. Secular, further, means the spirit of this age, these times, or the longest duration of this age and people living today. Luck as a secular faith, then, means a faith invested in this age, these times, or our own generation in contrast to the spiritual or eternal realities of faith in God or trust in providence.

Luck is confidence—that is, faith—in fate, in chance, in cleverness in figuring out probabilities. Gambling is a composite of the three. All are focused upon the immediate time situation, the here and now. All are distinctly dependent upon human existence apart from any fellowship with or interdependence upon the supernatural or the everlasting realities of life.

LUCK AND THE ETERNAL

Although we will examine the various facets of luck in more detail in the following chapters, let us look here at the relationship between luck and the eternal. The person who invests his or her faith in luck is locked into the present. For example, consider the gambler as one who trusts in luck. Although some gamblers calculate the probabilities and are willing to wait for a better chance, they are oblivious to the longer view of eternity.

In contrast, the Christian faith focuses upon the eternal. It relegates the event of the moment, whatever it may be, to insignificance. As Isaac Watts's hymn "O God, Our Help in Ages Past" says:

> A thousand ages in thy sight
> are like an evening gone.

In the presence of the eternal, even the skillful, mathematically expert calculator of the odds is trapped in the secularity of his or her fixation of faith in luck.

Along with this focus on the present, persons who invest their faith in luck often exhibit an undercurrent of contempt for work. They expect to get rich quickly without working. They do not heed even the wisdom of one generation, much less the everlasting wisdom of God. They assume that they can avoid the patient endurance and passage of time required in working for a living. A similar disregard for time and work was addressed by the apostle Paul. Some of the members of the Thessalonian church were refusing to come to terms with the passage of time. They believed so intently in the immediate return of the Lord that they refused to work. Paul laid down the admonition: "Anyone unwilling to work should not eat. For we hear that some of you are living in idleness, mere busybodies, not doing any work. Now such persons we command and exhort in the Lord Jesus Christ to do their work quietly and to earn their own living" (2 Thess. 3:10b–12).

In 1 Thessalonians 4:11–12, Paul also says, "Aspire to live quietly, to mind your own affairs, and to work with your hands . . . that you may behave properly toward outsiders and be dependent on no one."

A modern version of the person who dreams of "making a killing" in a very short time without working is the son or daughter of affluent parents. Such children sometimes assume that their parents have earned enough money in their lifetime to provide for their children without any effort on the part of the children. Such children talk of their dream of being a musician, entrepreneur, entertainer, or artist and becoming successful overnight. They are convinced that luck will bring their big opportunity without the endurance and discipline of time and effort, much less devotion to God.

The relation of work to the eternal is further illustrated in Paul's remarks after his lengthy discussion of the resurrection and what will be our nature in the resurrection. He said, "Therefore, my beloved, be steadfast, immovable, always excelling in the work of the Lord, because you know that in the Lord your labor is not in vain" (1 Cor. 15:58). He was speaking of not just work for work's sake to fill up meaningless time or to satisfy our acquisitive natures, but "the work of the Lord." Such activity is endowed not only with meaning and purpose for the believer, but it is also the nexus of a durable relationship to the Lord Jesus Christ who, in the days of his flesh, said, "We must work the works of him who sent me while it is day; night is coming when no one can work" (John 9:4).

Yet the believer in luck detaches work from its eternal setting and from a lasting relationship to the Lord Jesus Christ. Gambling can even become a reaction against work addiction in others as one challenges the important relationship between work and money. Some forms of work even become efforts to make an inordinate amount of money with a minimum amount of effort; such efforts lead to various forms of gambling, such as playing the stock market, investment in or betting on professional sports, and even some forms of religious ministry that push relentlessly for money by religious "marketing" through television promotion. Some religionists become what the apostle Paul called "peddlers of God's word" (2 Cor. 2:17). A religious entrepreneur may use the symbols of the eternal as a means of "sordid gain" or as a means of "lording it over" those in their charge (1 Peter 5:2–3). The symbols of the eternal are too holy to be used as means to such ends; they point to the eternal God.

In the activity I have just described, immediate gain and short-term satisfaction are the hallmarks of these forms of living by luck. Immediacy is a style of life that forgets and does not learn from the past. It does not consider the shape of things to come. The immediate moment is all that matters. The eternal and the ultimate outcome of the deeds of the present are not even considered. Therefore, the element of endurance that "produces character," as Paul says in Romans 5:4, is deleted from the formation of the person's personality. All is left to luck, not to the discipline of endurance or the dependable outcome of honest work. The personality that results is a dependent one at best, a narcissistic one at worst.

THE PROVIDENCE OF GOD

When a person is solely committed to the sagacious prediction of probabilities, he or she is trying to see ahead. The term *providence* literally means "to see ahead" (*vidēre,* "to see"; *pro,* "ahead"). Calculating the probabilities is a secularized form of providence. It raises the whole issue of luck as a secular form of providence in contradistinction from God the Creator and the Provider of our lives. An exploration of the meaning of providence in the Christian faith is therefore necessary.

The word *providence* is not used in the Old or New Testaments in the sense that Christians use it today. It is used only once in the King James Version. In that instance, Tertullus was a spokesman for Ananias, the high priest at the trial of the apostle Paul before Felix, the Roman procurator of Judea from A.D. 52 to A.D. 60. Tertullus flattered Felix in his introduction by saying: "Seeing that by thee we enjoy great quietness, and that very worthy deeds are done unto this nation by thy providence, we accept it always, and in all places, most noble Felix, with all thankfulness" (Acts 24:2–3, KJV). More recent translations, such as the New Revised Standard Version, use the word "foresight" in this passage.

However, the biblical understanding of the providence of God does not depend upon the use of the word. As William G. Pollard says:

> What to the faithful is an act of divine mercy showing forth our Lord's restorative power is for the pagan merely a piece of extraordinarily good luck. What to the faithful is a manifestation of divine judgment is to the pagan only a misfortune.[3]

Biblically and theologically, the providence of God has several meanings.

First, belief in the providence of God is the investment of one's faith in the work of God in our original creation. We are individuals both in terms of the gifts of our creation and in terms of the steadfastness of God's care of us in our personal history, our living present, and our hopes for the future. This is summarized in Romans 8:28: "We know that all things work together for good for those who love God, who are called according to his purpose." Dale Moody interprets this passage: "It is God who cooperates with the process of creation in human history, who brings good out of adverse situations and events. God, not things, has the last word on behalf of those who are called according to his purpose."[4]

Again, whereas luck as a secular faith is fixed on the present and the probabilities of the future, providence in a biblical sense is seen best in retrospect. Joseph, in the Old Testament story, was thrown into a pit by his brothers and then sold into slavery. He was then put into prison in Egypt. Finally, his situation changed. (Believers in luck would say that his big losing streak ended, and he began to win!) In fact, his dreams of his brothers and his father bowing down to him came true. In a dramatic flash of self-discovery, he recognized what God had been doing in the circumstances of his life. He had become the provider for his family. They were dependent upon his goodwill and his mercy. They survived by reason of *his* providence. But he attributed what had happened to God's providence and divested himself of the need to play God. He said to his brothers: "Do not be afraid! Am I in the place of God? Even though you intended to do harm to me, God intended it for good, in order to preserve a numerous people, as he is doing today" (Gen. 50:19–20). *God's* hidden providence now was suddenly revealed. Joseph saw it clearly as he looked back on his journey in life.

Thus, often providence is seen best in retrospect. The times of suffering in the pit and in prison certainly did not give Joseph even a fleeting glimpse of providence. Many of us in times of severe suffering are prone to ask: "What have I done to deserve this?" or, "Why is God punishing me so?" The passage of time reveals to us, as it did to Joseph, that God was preparing us to be God's provider for other people. Walter Brueggemann captures this perception of providence when he says: "By 'providence' I mean the hidden, patient, sovereign enactment of God's overriding purpose beyond the will and choice of human agents. . . . [O]ne does not want to credit everything to God or reduce God's providence to luck or good fortune."[5] In Joseph's case there was no magic or luck that enabled him to help his family in a twinkling of an eye. To the contrary, suffering, endurance, character, and hope sustained him over the pull of the years. Joseph in the pit and in prison experienced—retrospectively—the guiding of the providence of God.

Another perspective of providence, closely allied with the Joseph story, is that providence does not just mean "to see ahead." It means "to provide." In 1 Corinthians 10:13 Paul says: "No testing has overtaken you that is not common to everyone. God is faithful, and he will not let you be tested beyond your strength, but with the testing he will also provide the way out so that you may be able to endure it." Here the faithful God is the provider of the "way out." The story of Abraham about to offer up Isaac exemplifies this gift of God to us. Isaac, a boy old enough to carry the wood up the mountain for the sacrifice, asked his father, "The fire and the wood are here, but where is the lamb for a burnt offering?" In a statement of faith, Abraham answered, "God himself will provide the lamb for a burnt offering, my son" (Gen. 22:7–8). God did indeed deliver Isaac by providing a lamb. As Abraham hoped would happen, deliverance actually came to pass. Abraham named the mountain *Jehovah-Jireh,* which means "The Lord will provide."

Thus providence is not only "seeing ahead"; it is also the graciousness of God in providing "the way of escape" in the testing, tempting times of life. Therefore we can put our complete trust in God. If we do not, we become anxious and feel that we must manage and maneuver the probabilities through our own powers of control, trusting in luck. Jesus, however, taught that we can deal with anxiety in another way:

> "Therefore I tell you, do not worry about your life, what you will eat or what you will drink, or about your body, what you will wear. Is not life more than food, and the body more than clothing? Look at the birds of the air; they neither sow nor reap nor gather into barns, and yet your heavenly Father feeds them. Are you not of more value than they? . . . But strive first for the kingdom of God and his righteousness, and all these things will be given to you as well." (Matt. 6:25–26, 33)

This is not trusting in luck; rather, it is the disciplined seeking of the kingdom with serene trust in God.

Yet the working of God in our behalf is not always obvious and certainly not clear. As Brueggemann says: "The hidden caring of God is more difficult to speak about than the obvious, direct intrusions of God which we have come to call 'God's mighty acts.'" The mystery and hiddenness of God's providence cannot be explained. Brueggemann says further: "When everything is 'explained' life is denied and no new life imaginable. . . . [W]e are offered a new world in which God's providential care outruns both our remarkable personalities and our cunning, devastating power."[6]

Paul Tillich gives a remarkably clear summary of the activity of God in providence. He says:

> Providence is a *quality* of every constellation of conditions, a quality which drives or lures toward fulfillment. Providence is "the divine condition" which is present in every group of finite conditions and in the totality of finite conditions. . . . The man [or woman] who believes in providence does not believe special divine activity will alter the conditions of finitude and estrangement. He [or she] believes, and asserts with the courage of faith, that no situation whatsoever can frustrate the fulfillment of his [or her] ultimate destiny. That nothing can separate him [or her] from the love of God which is in Christ Jesus (Romans, chap. 8).[7]

The Providence of God in Jesus Christ

However, the veil of hiddenness of God is itself torn apart by the mighty act of God in the incarnation of Jesus Christ. This mighty act is the ultimate manifestation of the providence of God. Here the veil is removed in the human beingness of Jesus Christ. As the apostle Paul says, "And all of us, with unveiled faces, seeing the glory of the Lord as though reflected in a mirror, are being transformed into the same image from one degree of glory to another; for this comes from the Lord, the Spirit" (2 Cor. 3:18).

In the days of his flesh, Jesus did not leave anything to chance or luck. He was guided by the destiny for which he came into the world. He secured every situation because he was aware of the dangers to his life and to his disciples' lives. He left nothing to chance. He did not depend on luck. When he decided to go into Jerusalem for what we now call the triumphal entry, he told two of his disciples to go into the village ahead and, "as you enter it you will find tied there a colt that has never been ridden. Untie it and bring it here. If anyone asks you, 'Why are you untying it?' just say this, 'The Lord needs it'" (Luke 19:30–31). They did as he said, and it happened as he predicted. Accustomed as many are to imputing omniscience to Jesus in the days of his flesh, his directive looks like magic. However, a more likely explanation is that Jesus knew the owner of the colt and had an understanding with him. He had "fail-safed" the upcoming event.

The same kind of planning went into his arrangements for the Passover meal with his disciples. Jesus told them that when they entered the city, they would see a man carrying a jar of water.

> "Follow him into the house he enters and say to the owner of the house, 'The teacher asks you, "Where is the guest room, where I may eat the Passover with my disciples?"' He will show you a large room upstairs, already furnished. Make preparations for us there."

They found everything as Jesus had told them and prepared the Passover (Luke 22:10–13).

Preparation of seder, or the Passover meal, in a place where they would not be disturbed was no small task. It took advance planning. As tight as the security situation was for Jesus, again he did not leave these plans to chance or luck. He planned for them in minute detail. His care for his own and his disciples' safety expressed itself in carefulness. Fate, chance, probability, and gambling would be left to the disciple who betrayed him, the chief priests, and the Roman soldiers (who cast lots for his garments). He was led by the providence of God and did not trust any of these aspects of luck as a secular faith.

However, the most concrete descriptions of the way faith in God implements the intelligence of people are found in Jesus' wisdom and ethical teachings about the foolish person. He tells of the wise person who builds a house upon rock and the foolish person who builds a house on sand (Matt. 7:24–27). He describes the lack of preparations of the foolish maidens and the wisdom of the prepared ones as the time of meeting the bridegroom approached (Matt. 25:1–13). Wisdom in making decisions that will stand the test of time and wisdom in being prepared for clearly known eventualities is the opposite of leaving things to chance or luck. Wisdom consists of using the intelligence God has given us. Foolishness is leaving this gift of intelligence unused.

Leslie Weatherhead, pastor of City Temple Church in London during Hitler's bombing of the city, says: "How would mankind learn anything if his foolishness, carelessness, stupidity and ignorance were always overcome" by the omnipotence of God. "To prevent, by a use of omnipotence, foolishness from producing its consequences would fill the earth with unteachable fools."[8]

The fool is also the object of Jesus' remonstrance. Jesus pointed to the foolishness of the Pharisees who cleaned the outside of the dish but left the inside unclean. He told them they were filled with extortion and wickedness. He said: "You fools! Did not the one who made the outside make the inside also? So give for alms those things that are within; and see, everything will be clean for you" (Luke 11:40–41). He also tells the story of the rich fool to whom God said: "You fool! This very night your life is being demanded of you. And the things you have prepared, whose will they be?" (Luke 12:20). In contemporary psychiatric appraisals, thinking like that of the rich fool is called "impaired judgment." However, the judgment as to who is a fool and who is not is not ours to make. In Matthew 5:22 Jesus warns, "If you say, 'You fool,' you will be liable to the hell of fire." That judgment is a prerogative of God and not the judgment of people upon one another.

The Mystery of the Providence of God

Even with the full disclosure of God's being in Jesus Christ, still God in Christ moves in mysterious ways wonders to perform. The apostle Paul wrote: "We speak God's wisdom, secret and hidden, which God decreed before the ages for our glory. . . . 'What no eye has seen, nor ear heard, nor the human heart conceived, what God has prepared for those who love him'" (1 Cor. 2:7, 9).

To begin the life of faith in the face of such awesome mystery is not ordinarily done by carefully reasoning out the intricacies of the mysteries of God. To the contrary, one is energized by the mysteries of God in Christ to take the leap of faith. One does not calculate the probabilities, assess the chances, or move fatalistically. One places his or her life in the care and providence of God in a total commitment, free of the anxiety of which Jesus spoke.

RISK AND THE LIFE OF FAITH

Such a faith is one of adventure and risk in the sure knowledge of the presence of God. An example is Albert Schweitzer, a physician, authority on Bach, and premier organist. He left Europe and set up a hospital in the Lambarene in Africa. His move was an adventuresome risk into the unknown. Nevertheless, he took the risk and ministered to people who otherwise would not have medical care. In the course of doing so he also produced several philosophical and religious works that challenged the contemporary interpretations of the Gospels.

A friend and colleague of mine, a business man, turned down a position in the upper echelons of power in the United States Senate. Instead he took a position as a representative of a multinational corporation that gives him full permission to do his lay ministry with the people of Thailand and Malaysia. His home church wants to ordain him as a representative of his denomination. He does not feel that this is for him. He thinks it would be an impediment in relating to Thais and Malaysians if he were an official representative of an American church. He prefers that all risks be his own.

When we think of the life of faith and risk, we find an interface between luck as a secular faith, with its calculation of probabilities, and the life of faith in God in Jesus Christ. The whole sphere of calculation of possibilities is now part of the world of science. As Roger Shinn says, "In the contemporary world science provides much of the information for making policy decisions." He quotes Immanuel Kant's aphorism: "Faith without science is silent; science without faith is aimless." He further says:

> The Christian meets the world with the Bible in one hand, the daily newspaper in the other. Both hands are essential; neither alone is adequate. The Bible represents faith, a loyalty, a commitment coming out of a heritage, but it does not tell contemporary believers what to do in all situations faced. The newspaper represents what is happening in the world today. It does not probe the meaning of all that happens that will direct readers in responding to events.[9]

Together the two provide data and the meaning of the data.

However, scientists sometimes proceed without humility and become devoid of interest in the philosophical and religious response to their findings. They can be like the Pharisees and Sadducees who asked Jesus to show them a sign from heaven. He replied: "When it is evening, you say, 'It will be fair weather, for the sky is red.' And in the morning, 'It will be stormy today, for the sky is red and threatening.' You know how to interpret the appearance of the sky, but you cannot interpret the signs of the times" (Matt. 16:2–3). A science in dialogue with the life of faith, to the contrary, searches the meaning of discoveries before God. This improves upon the fatalism of a purely secular quest into the probabilities and chances of meaningless information and results.

LONELINESS AND THE SPIRITUAL COMMUNITY

The luck-driven person seems to live in the spirit of fatalism and self-sufficiency. The degree of existential loneliness such a person carries is rarely articulated, even as the awareness that luck is her or his faith is also inarticulated. Such a person may share the feeling Coleridge describes in *The Rime of the Ancient Mariner:*

> Alone, alone, all, all alone,
> Alone on a wide wide sea!
> And never a saint took pity on
> My soul in agony.[10]

This loneliness is apparent in the life of the gambler, our exemplar of the one who lives by the secular faith in luck. The gambler in the casino and the gambler in the storefront lottery both live an isolated existence. The operators of the casino or the lottery may seem to have a relationship with each other within the bureaucratic organization. But like many bureaucracies, these are not fellowships of people who care for each other and are committed to each other in a community of faith. These are what Martin Buber calls collectivities,

> not a binding but a bundling together; individuals packed together, armed and equipped in common, with only as much life from man to man as will inflame the marching step. . . . Collectivity is based upon an atrophy of personal existence, community on its increase and confirmation in life lived towards one another.[11]

The game of bingo can be a community of fun-loving people, gathered together in a mutual commitment to some charitable cause, usually a church fellowship. However, this sense of community is missing among the gamblers in the bingo hall. In bingo, more often than not, the isolation and loneliness of the gambler abound. It is said that more people become addicted to bingo than to other kinds of gambling. The connection between loneliness and assuagement in any addiction is unmistakable and readily apparent.

In the life of the spiritual community, people can bind themselves together in a community of faith in God and in both God's hidden and obvious providence. Such a church can be as Thomas Helwys says in his confession of about 1612: "That the members of every church or congregation ought to know one another, that so they may perform all the duties of love towards one another both to soul and body."[12] Churches today meet the need of members to know one another by forming small, face-to-face groups of people who know each other and do the works of love toward each other. These may be study groups or support groups of persons suffering the same kinds of tribulation, such as grief, divorce, substance abuse, or an emotional disorder such as depression. They may be task force groups focused on the care of the sick, ministry to disabled and shut-in people, or ministry to new people who have come to the larger community and are "strangers within the gates" of the community.

Whatever kind of fellowship it is and for whatever purpose, one of the central effects of the group is to do away with loneliness, provide a sense of belonging, and offer a fellowship of fellow burden bearers. This is the distinctly human, horizontal, existential aspect of such a fellowship.

THE PRESENCE AND
PROVIDENCE OF THE LIVING GOD

The divine, vertical, and eternal dimension of this fellowship is the presence and providence of the living God. Even in the darkest of human suffering and the worst of human "luck," faith in this God provides us with an eternal Paraclete, one who comes alongside us (see John 14:15–17, which uses "Advocate" in the NRSV). Thus God's providence provides us with what Paul Tillich has termed the "courage to be" in the face of the threats to our existence. This God is constant, as over against the fickleness of fate. This God is reliable in the chance and risk of our daily existence. God enables us to face with serenity the probabilities of an uncertain future. We can still think of having "the best luck" or the "worst luck" in given situations. But faith in luck is not the substance of our being. The substance of our faith is in the steadfast love and constant providence of the living God. Allusions to luck in a given situation are merely humorous ways of easing the tension of life along with our friends. Luck is not faith but fun in the face of the absurdities of life.

Our faith is in the person and the transformation of life made possible daily by the presence and teachings of our Lord Jesus Christ. We are not anxious about the probabilities of tomorrow. The uncertainties of the day are enough to thrust us upon God's presence and providence. Now let us take a long hard look at the inner and outer nature of luck as a secular faith.

2. Driving Forces of the Belief in Luck

*W*hen we speak of faith—especially of a secular faith in luck—we ordinarily are referring to a belief system. That belief system may be conscious or unconscious, articulate or inarticulate. In either instance, the belief in luck is energized by several forces. In this chapter, let us examine some of these driving forces of the secular faith in luck.

RESPONDING TO CHAOS

Some of our experience of the created order of the universe has a specific, reliable, and predictable nature. We can count on the sun rising and setting and the regularity of the tides of the seas. We know that the seasons in temperate climates are reliable and in tropical zones are at times hardly noticeable. The sun, the moon, and the stars follow their predictable orbits. However, much of our human contact with the world is anything but orderly, predictable, and reliable. Rather, it is chaotic, filled with disorder and pandemonium. Earthquakes, hurricanes, tornadoes, volcanic eruptions, and land- and snowslides are only minimally predictable. These wreak havoc and chaos upon anyone in their path. The orders and doctrines of creation neither predict nor control them. They are nature and life gone amok.

As Paul Tillich says:

> Creation and chaos belong to each other, and even the exclusive monotheism of biblical religion confirms this structure of life. It is echoed in its symbolic descriptions of the divine life, of its abysmal depth, of its suffering with its creatures, of its destructive wrath. But in the divine life the element of chaos leads to the ambiguity of self-creativity and destruction.[1]

This concurrence of creation and chaos is found in biblical thinking. John Pederson documents the coexistence of the Creator God and chaos. The wilderness is "a cursed country where blessing is lacking. The wilderness is the land of chaos . . . the lawless, and the empty." He quotes Isaiah 34:11a: "He shall stretch the line of confusion over it, and the plummet of chaos over its nobles." Pederson further says: "The fight of Yahweh against the ocean of chaos . . . is sometimes described as a fight with the dragon, *Tannin,* called by the name of Rahab and Leviathan and surrounded by helpers" (see Job 9:13).[2]

Today, with secularization at flood stage, no such mythology is alive in the Western mind to help us reconcile the chaos of nature and the order of a Creator. Rather, faith in luck is the means used by many to push back the confusion and mystery of chaos. In contemporary popular thinking, the realm of chaos in nature—or "life"—is clearly secularized and neatly held apart from the thought of God. The compartmentalization of the chaotic events of life apart from God's action in the world is expressed in Robert Schuller's bonny optimism: "Life is not fair, but God is good." Thus life is left with a vacuum of meaning. Popular belief in good and especially bad luck rushes in to fill the vacuum. The very real encounter with chaos becomes one of the driving forces in the secular faith in luck in the face of the ambiguity posed by chaos in human life.

The person who lives in the presence of the chaos in life can face the hazards we have mentioned with a "good luck/bad luck" attitude, "taking chances" that the odds will be in his or her favor. One's life becomes more serene, however, if these chaotic situations are faced with an intelligent attention to the inherent dangers of life combined with an abiding confidence in the providence that God in Jesus Christ is with one in either the event of trouble or the deliverance from trouble. As William Cowper says in his hymn "God Moves in a Mysterious Way":

> Judge not the Lord by feeble sense,
> But trust him for his grace;
> Behind a frowning providence
> He hides a smiling face.[3]

Providence is seen more clearly *after* the deliverance from destruction than during chaos' fury. In retrospect, the "smiling face" is amazingly evident.

The secular faith in luck often coexists alongside a pietistic Christian faith. A vivid example of this paradox came to light in relation to the running of the 1992 Kentucky Derby, the epitome of ritualized faith in luck. The French horse, Arazi, was the heavy favorite, with $1,103,548 having been bet upon him at post time. He had the post position of number 17, putting him at a handicap. Instead of winning the race, he came in eighth in the finale.

The race was won by a little-known horse, Lil E. Tee, with a post position of number 10, a distinct advantage over Arazi. Lil E. Tee was ridden by jockey Pat Day, the all-time winner of money at Churchill

Downs, the legendary site of the Kentucky Derby, for the last eighteen years. However, he had never before won a Kentucky Derby race, the next to the last race on Derby Day, the first Saturday in May. Yet by all counts, Pat Day was the most skillful jockey since Willie Shoemaker and Eddie Arcaro.

Pat Day is a born-again Christian. Yet he said, "I knew there was a Derby out there with my name on it." This is a "faith-in-luck" statement. He also is a Shriner. He vowed that if he won, he would wear his Shriner's hat at the victory circle presentation, and he did. This is a lucky "fetish" behavior. Yet as he rode into the circle to have the blanket of roses placed on Lil E. Tee's neck, he said, "All things work together for good for those who love the Lord Jesus." This is a paraphrase of Romans 8:28: "We know that all things work together for good for those who love God, who are called according to his purpose." In this Pat Day gave praise to God for his victory. What a remarkable coexistence of faith in luck and faith in God! It would be cynical indeed to expect Pat Day at such an exhilarating moment in his life to keep these elements neatly separate. We can best find companionship with him in the ways in which we ourselves blend our Christian faith with our secular faith in luck.

This coexistence of the belief in luck with living religions is true not only of Christianity. Taoism, for example, leaves no room for luck, as is apparent in the following famous parable of the *Old Man at the Fort:*

> An old man was living with his son at an abandoned fort on top of a hill, and one day he lost a horse. The neighbors came to express their sympathy for this misfortune, and the Old Man asked, "How do you know this is bad luck?" A few days later his horse returned with a number of wild horses and his neighbors came again to congratulate him on this stroke of fortune, and the Old Man replied, "How do you know this is good luck?" With so many horses around, his son took to riding, and one day he broke his leg. Again the neighbors came around to express their sympathy, and the Old Man replied, "How do you know this is bad luck?" The next year, there was a war, and because the Old Man's son was crippled, he did not have to go to the front.[4]

However, even though classical Taoism held to the futility of belief in luck, as this parable illustrates, nevertheless the marketplace life of the Chinese held to a secular belief in luck. Christina Chang, a Chinese colleague of mine, gave me a talisman that Chinese hang on the wall of many Chinese homes, which says: "Follow your fate. Everything is arranged by fate." This is a very common saying among Buddhists. The very prevalent Chinese idea is that everybody comes into the world with a certain amount of luck or happiness. If one enjoys too much of something, he or she uses up luck in other areas of life. A friend, Keith Luse, a businessman with a multinational corporation, sent me a clipping from a Bangkok, Thailand, newspaper, *The Nation*. It describes the political campaign for prime minister of Chatichoi Chooshaven, a leader of one of the political parties. Commenting on another party leader's suitability for the office in spite of charges of corruption, Chooshaven said of the chances of a veteran politician being made prime minister: "It depends on chance and your own luck."[5] This is congruent with the belief that each person has his or her own luck quotient. On the same front page is a picture of an automobile wreck captioned "Monks in lucky escape!"

One group of four Chinese women were horrified by the atrocities of the Japanese invasion in the 1930s and 1940s. These women asked: "How much can you wish for a warm coat that hangs in the closet of a house that burned down with your mother and father in it? How long can you see in your mind arms and legs hanging from telephone wires and starving dogs running down the street with half-chewed hands dangling from their mouths?"

Such chaos created terror in their hearts. They had a choice. They could sit and contemplate such horrors with somber faces, or they could "choose their own happiness." Therefore, the four women chose to organize a club. They met once a week over the best meal they could prepare. They played games and told good stories that made them "laugh to death." They could win ten thousand *yuan* and still not have anything because toilet paper was worth more than paper money! "That made us laugh harder, to think that a thousand *yuan* note wasn't even good enough to rub on our bottoms." They chose their own luck— to laugh at the absurdity and ambiguity of the world around them. They made their own luck in the midst of the disaster of war. They named their weekly parties the Joy Luck Club.[6]

THE AMBIGUITY OF LIFE

Chaos in the presence of a religious or a scientific belief in the orderliness of God's creation plunges us into a poignant sense of the ambiguity in life. The devout Christian holds firmly to the compassionate understanding of God as that God is revealed in the face and person of Jesus Christ. Yet the inherent injustices in life, such as the deaths of "the Galileans whose blood Pilate had mingled with their sacrifices . . . [o]r those eighteen who were killed when the tower of Siloam fell on them" (Luke 13:1, 4), present us with an ambiguous incongruity. Those suffering such tragedies were the unlucky ones, even the most devout are likely to say and believe. Thus we attempt to deal with two contradictory aspects of the real world in our thinking. Such tragedies are chance events, unfortunate happenings, the "fell clutch of circumstance"—bad luck. To believe that they are such simplifies the ambiguity. Belief in luck becomes a way of explaining and living with chance and the accidents of life.

The hazards of human life are innumerable. Daily living is a risky pursuit. Both consciously and without thinking, people take risks: in the food we eat, in the automobiles and planes in which we travel, in the noxious fumes we breathe, to name a few. Therefore, one of the driving forces of our belief in luck is the courage it gives us to take the risks we do.

We "trust our luck" in the face of many kinds of risks. Some risks are inadvertent, as in the case of accidents of all kinds to which we are subject. Other instances of bad luck are the results of malicious vandals, as in the case of someone slitting the tires of our automobile. Other risks are obvious and near at hand, whereas some risks are hidden and more remote. The risks of drunken driving are plainly seen in the here and now. The risks of cigarette smoking are more insidious and remote. The risks of global warming because of the gradual destruction of the ozone layer are remote enough to be debatable at our leisure. The number of deaths in a plane crash captures the headlines and rivets the attention of the populace, whereas the same number of deaths in automobile crashes captures little notice. One risk is spectacular; the other is subtle and chronic.[7]

In these events we take either unthinking, impulsive, or calculated risks. In all instances, we are trusting our luck. Belief in luck is driven by our need to take risks. The more calculated the risk we take, the more forceful is the belief in luck driven by the calculation. The calculation introduces the scientific process of estimating the probability of either good luck or bad luck occurring. As we will see in chapter 6, gambling is a deliberate manipulation of the probability of gain or loss, good luck or bad luck.

Yet this is a coldly impersonal way of living life. One characteristic of a secular faith in luck in a world filled with chaos is that the person who lives this way is surrounded by the loneliness of life. As Gardner Murphy, at one time a research psychologist at the Menninger Clinic, said: "In a future psychology of personality there will surely be a place for directly grappling with [our] response to the cosmos, [our] sense of unity with it, the nature of [our] demands upon it, and [our] *feeling of loneliness or consummation* (italics mine) in [our] contemplation of it."[8]

That loneliness is not assuaged by a secular faith in luck. Faith in God does away with the loneliness and creates a fellowship with God in searching for meaning in the mysterious chaos of the universe and companionship in facing the chaos of the threat of the unknown (see chapter 1).

MYSTERY AND BELIEF IN LUCK

The universe and our daily lives in it are filled with mystery. As O. T. Binkley, my esteemed professor and lifelong mentor, once said, "I wonder how long it will be until I know half as much as I don't know." Mystery is that which is a hidden or secret thing, a matter unexplained or inexplicable, beyond human knowledge or comprehension. Rudolf Otto still remains the authentic voice on the meaning and nature of mystery. We can use his interpretation of mystery to understand mystery as a driving force in the belief in luck. All the while we must recognize that Otto himself does not make the connection between the mysterious and luck.

Otto bypasses the rational descriptions of God at the same time that he insists that these are necessary. Yet they are inadequate expressions of the Holy, or, if one believes so, God. To stop at the rational requires that persons shut their eyes to that which is unique in religious experience. He affirms the numinous, the numen, or the Holy, characterized by a nonrational, "creature feeling." In our creatureliness, we experience the numinous in two dimensions of mystery: the *mysterium tremendum* and the *mysterium fascinans*. Otto interprets these in terms of the experience of God.[9] However, his analyses can be used to interpret both religious and secular aspects of human belief and behavior.

The Uncanny and the Belief in Luck

The *mysterium tremendum* prompts three responses. The first is awfulness, in which a person shudders at the strange, new, and that which "has no place in the everyday natural or ordinary experience." Second is the feeling of being overpowered. One dares not approach the mysterium. If one marshals the courage to approach it, there is a "feeling of impotence and general nothingness as against overpowering might, dirt and ashes against majesty." It is the feeling of Isaiah when he said, "Woe is me! I am lost" (Isa. 6:5). "Third, the element of energy or urgency is inspired by . . . and it clothes itself in symbolical expressions—vitality, passion, emotional temper, will, force, movement, excitement, activity, impetus."[10]

However, the believer in luck faces this mysterium as a pawn of fate, hoping only that the odds or chance is with and not against him or her. Isaiah faced the same mysterium as an expression of Yahweh's holiness. He persevered by faith in the intensely personal providence of Yahweh. He received a personal sense of mission in response to Yahweh's question "Who will go for us?"

These responses to the *mysterium tremendum*—awfulness, the feeling of being overpowered, and the incursion of energy and vitality—are the characteristics of the worship of the Holy. However, the secular minded, functioning without any sense of God's reality, may interpret the same feelings quite differently in response to the mysterious elements in life.

Harry Stack Sullivan describes very similar emotions, which he calls the experience of the uncanny. The sense of the uncanny creates anxiety reactions of awe, dread, loathing, and horror, not at all unlike Otto's description of responses to the *mysterium tremendum*.[11]

The Uncanny and the Foreboding of the Future

One of the greatest anxieties we experience is the anxiety of the unknown. We feel the depth of anxiety in the present and extended anxiety as we look to the future. In the present we may have a sense of awe, dread, loathing, and horror in the fear of the unknown dimensions of a disease we have or of a business transaction in which our total financial security is at stake. Apart from any sense of the sacred, this sense of the uncanny takes the form of the belief in good or bad luck, a secular faith.

Anxiety about the future can also be filled with a sense of foreboding, dread, and even loathing and horror. These responses may lead us to look for omens and to make an attempt to "psych out" the shape of the future. The rituals of psyching out the future are fortune-telling rituals. The secular faith in luck prompts some people to seek out fortune tellers. They consult persons who ostensibly have the gift of being psychic. These mystic messengers use playing cards, crystals, tarot, and other avenues as focus points to attune the person's "vibrational energies" in which they professedly receive images. They advertise: "Let us help you understand your life—past, present, and future! Call for an appointment! Ask for Ana! Donations only $20."

More overt expressions of such magical manipulations can be observed in the New Age shops in Santa Monica and Los Angeles, California. Streets are lined with shops selling garnets, amulets, rocks, and crystals for a sanitized primitive magic. New Age psychotherapists—even trained in clinical psychology—add to their training the use of crystals for producing mystical and magical spells on their clients.

Even in a rural church in the bluegrass section of Kentucky, church members told me, with no sense of incongruity with their faith in Christ, of having regularly consulted fortune-tellers.

Others will turn to occult practices such as communicating with the dead through mediums often called necromancers. A biblical example of turning to the occult is that of Saul. Samuel had died and was no longer a mentor for Saul. "Saul had expelled the mediums and the wizards from the land." Then the Philistines encamped against Saul and Israel. Saul was "afraid, and his heart trembled greatly." When he "inquired of the LORD, the LORD did not answer" either by dreams, by Urim, or by prophets (Urim was a sacred object consulted for answers on crucial issues). None of these answered Saul. Then Saul disobeyed his own laws and consulted the medium of Endor. He was disguised, and she did not know him. He promised her that no punishment would come to her. He asked that she call up the spirit of Samuel, who predicted Saul's death at the hands of the Philistines (1 Sam. 28:1–25). In consulting the medium, Saul did an evil thing before God.

The Uncanny and Magic

Rudolf Otto says that the "mystery" also "shows itself as something attractive and fascinating. . . . [T]he 'mystery' is . . . not merely something to be wondered at but something that entrances."[12] He names this the *mysterium fascinans.* He associates this both with the grace of high religious experience and with the more primitive attempts to master the mysterious, to manipulate the uncanny dimension of human experience.

One form of the latter is the good luck/bad luck belief and practice in magic. By this I do not mean the various tricks performed in a show for a fun-seeking audience. I am referring here to magic that aims to influence the mysterious forces of a person's life toward good luck and away from bad luck. Otto says that, far from the pursuit of the Holy, this is "profane goods pursued by magic." And as Samuel Southard says:

> Magic is based on the belief that supernatural powers will do what we want them to do. Of course, we must find a man or woman who knows about these powers, or learn from someone how to say the right words or perform the right acts to get what we want. But once we have the right words or acts, we are sure to bring the powers under our direction.

In East Asia, "bomahs or *pawangs* are important members of the community regarded as knowledgeable and having power with the forces of nature and spirits that inhabit the unseen world. They make use of spells, charms, potions, talismans, etc., to mediate between living men and the forces and spirits that surround and influence them."[13]

Such personalities as the bomah or *pawangs* are not found among the cultural leaders of American communities. However, there are leaders of occult groups that are subcultures in their own right in this country. In the culturally sophisticated segments of American life, many of the originators of the nearly three hundred forms of psychotherapy are endowed with hidden assumptions of their magic power by those who seek their help. They are gurus in many senses of the word. A few of these forms of psychotherapy, such as cognitive therapy and classical psychoanalytic therapy, have stood the test of double-blind research to validate or invalidate the outcome of their therapy. However, many of these forms of therapy are quite dependent upon the charisma of their inventors and the success these persons have had in attracting followers. The human potential movement of the sixties has given birth to a wide variety of groups that seek to enhance one's "chances" at a better life. Some of these are Esalen, EST (Erhard Seminars Training), rebirthing therapy, and transcendental meditation.

WHEN LIFE IS UNFAIR

In a world in which life is too often uncertain, belief in luck reinforces a popular stoicism that enables people to live a life unperturbed by the misfortunes and unfairness of life. Such a popular stoicism, or marketplace stoicism, is not the classical stoicism of Marcus Aurelius and others that we will be considering in the next chapter. The burgeoning underclass in American society is imbued with this popular stoicism. One of the reasons is that we are undergoing a technological revolution that is leaving poorly educated and unskilled labor as "surplus," expendable humanity who are harassed and helpless like sheep without a shepherd. They feel that their desires for a better life are being repressed by the force of law and order. Ordinarily, luck, a secular faith, calms their fears and keeps alive the flickers of their hopes. When faith in luck fails them, they easily revert to violence, protesting the hopelessness of their lot in life.

Such a protest was one factor in the massive riots, killings, and burnings of Los Angeles in the spring of 1992. Some in the underclass resorted to violence to make their own luck. Politicians have tended to blame first one person or group, then another. It is obvious that everyone's luck has run out in the many violent events of this century.

The apostle Paul recognizes that the unfairness of life causes "tribulation" or "suffering." He introduces his discussion with a forthright affirmation that "since we are justified by faith, we have peace with God through our Lord Jesus Christ, through whom we have obtained access to this grace in which we stand; and we boast in our hope of sharing the glory of God" (Rom. 5:1–2). He assumes the unfairness of life, that the rain falls upon just and the unjust impartially. The word he uses, which is translated "suffering" in the New Revised Standard Version, can be translated "tribulation," or "trouble," or "affliction," or "oppression," or "persecution." Paul "boasts" in the suffering experienced, "knowing that suffering produces endurance, and endurance produces character, and character produces hope, and hope does not disappoint us, because God's love has been poured into our hearts through the Holy Spirit that has been given to us" (Rom. 5:3–5).

Endurance of the common lot of unfairness in life seems to begin the process of entertaining hope in the face of the inequities of life. Our standing in Christ is sustained by the steady providence of God that enables us to endure the tribulations a day at a time. As Jesus said, "Today's trouble is enough for today" (Matt. 6:34). Hope seems to be the major difference between fatalism and Christian hope based on dependence on providence.

3. Fatalism

A person may experience one tragic event in life after another. If so, he or she may feel fated or destined to have bad luck. Or, to the contrary, a person may have a sense of destiny that causes her or him to believe that no matter what happens, negative or positive, she or he will survive, persist, endure until all turns out for the good in the long run. Both of these attitudes reflect a style of life that is pervaded by fate-filled assumptions. Fatalism, then, is the assumption that one has no control over what happens in life. One simply must put up with whatever life brings.

Fatalism is one form of luck. Fate means that our lot is cast at the outset of our lives. One version of this view, a position espoused by Plato, is that we are free to choose, but we are fated by our choices. However, this is a milder form of fatalism. Fate in its purest form is an unerring determinism. Our lot is ours to bear, an arbitrary destiny that is set. We must endure it.

In this sense, fatalism is either submission to the inevitable negative happenings or elation at the inevitable positive happenings in life. Fatalism is the doctrine that the occurrence of all things is necessitated by the nature of things or by the fixed or inevitable decree of the arbiters of nature, the fates.

Therefore, let us survey from several angles what fatalism is about and the ways it has been expressed throughout the centuries and continues its influence today.

FATALISM IN GREEK
AND ROMAN THOUGHT

In Greek religion, the goddesses of fate, or destiny, were called the Moirai; they determined the course of human life. The three individual goddesses of the Moirai were (1) Clotho (the Spinner), who spins the thread of life; (2) Lachesis (the Disposer of Fate), who determines the length of life; and (3) Atropos (Inflexible), who cuts life off in death. (The Roman names of these goddesses are Nona, Decuma, and Morta.) In later Greek tradition, these goddesses gave rise to the picture of three old women: one who spun out people's destinies, one who drew them out over the life span, and the other who cut people's destinies off in death.

Plato vividly describes the human spirit as preexisting this life. He says that our destiny is not allotted to us but that we *choose* our genius, the life that we chose as our destiny. However, the lots themselves are spun "on the knees of necessity" by goddesses "three in number, each sitting upon her throne: these are the Fates, daughters of Necessity . . . Lachesis, and Clotho, and Atropos. . . Lachesis singing of the past, Clotho of the present, Atropos of the future."[1]

Today these goddesses are only occasionally worshiped in cults as such, but the belief in fate is very much in force. The past is deified in behavioral scientists' determinism focused on heredity in the DNA and the changeless impact of childhood development on the rest of life. The elements of chance in the present are epitomized in the statistical odds associated with disease, accidents, and unpredictable occurrences. The future is divined by astrology, various forms of fortune telling, gambling, computer projection, and poll taking. The harshest form of fatalism leaves no room for chance or freedom in the life of people or in the universe, in the acts of God, in the natural order or in the unfolding of history.

Stoicism, a Greek school of thought founded by Zeno, a Phoenician from Cyprus (ca. 335–263 B.C.), was still widely followed during the time of the apostle Paul. The Stoics brought light and wisdom to the fatalism of their day. Marcus Aurelius (121–180 A.D.) makes this clear:

> For two reasons it is right to be content with that which happens to thee because it was done for thee and prescribed for thee, and in a manner had reference to thee, originally from the most ancient causes spun thy destiny; and the other reason because even that which comes severally to every man is to the power which administers the universe a cause of felicity and perfection, nay even its continuance.[2]

Aurelius not only urges his readers to be content with their lot, but says that to do so maintains the order of creation undisturbed. Thus fatalism becomes a person's contentment with his or her lot in life. Contentment, Aurelius seems to say, arises from the imperturbability of the human soul. "Things do not touch the human soul, not in the least degree," he says, "nor . . . can they turn or move the human soul, but the soul moves itself alone, and whatever judgments it may think proper to make, and makes for itself the things which present themselves to it."[3] Hence the human spirit is by nature imperturbable.

In Aurelius's Stoicism, fate is that which is our human lot and can be met by a soul that cannot be touched by happenings. A modern version of this attitude is found in William E. Henley's "Invictus":

> Out of the night that covers me,
>   Black as the Pit from pole to pole,
> I thank whatever gods may be
>   For my unconquerable soul.
>
> In the fell clutch of circumstance,
>   I have not winced nor cried aloud:
> Under the bludgeoning of chance
>   My head is bloody, but unbowed.
>
> Beyond this place of wrath and tears
>   Looms the horror of the shade,
> And yet the menace of the years
>   Finds, and shall find me unafraid.
>
> It matters not how strait the gate,
>   How charged with punishments the scroll,
> I am the master of my fate:
>   I am the captain of my soul.[4]

Henley's dark fatalism is filled with self-sufficiency and loneliness. Yet he persists in the confidence that he can overcome circumstances. In this respect, his thought is somewhat more optimistic than that of the Stoics. The wise person, according to Stoicism as indicated by Marcus Aurelius, will be impervious to pain and pleasure, to wealth and poverty, to success and misfortune. That person will be fortified against all the slings of fortune from external circumstances by an impenetrable armor of imperturbability.

A distinctly Christian version of this attitude appears in the teaching of the apostle Paul in Philippians 4:11–12. He has learned to be content in facing hunger and plenty, abundance and want.

> Not that I am alluding to want, for I have learned to find resources in myself whatever my circumstances. I know what it is to be brought low, and I know what it is to have plenty. I have been very thoroughly initiated into the human lot with all its ups and downs—fullness and hunger, plenty and want. (Phil. 4:11–12, NEB)

If one stops reading here, one would say that Paul is at least a Stoic fatalist. However, he attributes his ability to be content to his very personal relationship with Christ: "I have strength for anything through him who gives me power" (Phil. 4:13, NEB). He also refers to the community of faith who have revived their concern for him. "You did care about me before for that matter; it was opportunity that you lacked" (Phil. 4:10, NEB). One of the differences between secular fatalists and believers in the providence of God is the self-sufficiency of the fatalist and reliance upon the fellowship and community of faith of fellow sufferers.

Adherents of classical Stoicism built their faith on a broad base of philosophical belief. They believed in the *Logos,* an eternal wisdom guiding the universe and a divine spark in each person. They believed in a blending of natural law and reason. The exercise of reason in the knowledge of natural law enabled a person to live according to wisdom—not chance or luck—and to maintain a serenity and imperturbability in the face of all circumstances of life.

Marketplace stoicism today is not this spiritually informed or disciplined. To the contrary, this attitude views life as a string of things that just happen. "Life is just one d____d thing after another" is the colloquial saying that captures the fatalism of the marketplace stoic. People move on the assumption that life is unfair and that the severe adversities of their life are to-be-expected bad luck, as we noted in the last chapter. This outlook on life is especially prevalent in the minds of people of the underclass of poverty and the working poor. Feeling helpless to control events and to make things happen in behalf of themselves and loved ones, they live from one reversal of fortune to another. Their apathy is spawned by helplessness. They live each day with little hope for the future, with no goals beyond surviving a day at a time. As Karen Bloomquist quotes one working class person: "When you work day in and day out at a job . . . like typing or packing ping pong paddles . . . the contraction, the listlessness, the absence of that spark comes to seem like a natural part of your character."[5]

However, the working poor have a usually unrecognized belief in luck as they face the boredom and the treadmill existence of their work. They dream of "hitting it big," of coming into wealth when a distant uncle's estate is settled. Or they dutifully return the forms of the Publishers' Clearinghouse Sweepstakes. More often they invest five or ten dollars a week in the lottery. Some of them become addicted to forms of legalized gambling, hoping for the ever-receding pot of gold at the end of the rainbow of good luck. Corporations and state governments bleed these trapped ones of what little money they have. The idea of investing five or ten dollars a week in a savings account seems too dull, boring, and unexciting for these victims of the dream of "hitting it big." Yet such a generalization overlooks the presence of vigorous hope on the part of the Christian working poor. A hard-nosed realism fills their lives. They invest their hopes in their children, whom they want to have a better life than they themselves have had. They invest their hope in the providence of God and a prudent poverty and discipline. They are not dreamers and bettors in life.

The underclass of poverty often have a source of hope that the affluent do not have—their fellowship of suffering, comfort, and hope found in their church. God as the source of hope sustains them. This communion of care, which often takes the boredom and treadmill apathy out of their lives, is a support that some working rich do not even know they do not have! Hope is part of the answer to the hopelessness and ennui of life.

FATE AS SCIENTIFIC
AND SECULAR DETERMINISM

Marcus Aurelius stated succinctly the core philosophy of fate in scientific determinism. "That which happens to (or suits) every man is fixed in a manner suitable to his destiny."[6] Benedict de Spinoza (1632–77) said that things "are determined to existence and action in a fixed and prescribed manner."[7] He also said that God determines everything, and "a thing which has been determined by God to any action cannot render itself indeterminate."[8] Sir Isaac Newton (1642–1727) spoke of the Creator as "the counsel of an intelligent agent" in ordering the universe. "He created them and set them in order. . . . [B]eing once formed, it may continue by those laws for ages." These thinkers ascribed to God the determined nature of the universe and our being. Though "blind fate," as Newton called it, "could never make all the planets move in one and the same way," nevertheless this was the work of "the counsel of an intelligent" God.[9] Though they were believers in God, nevertheless their scientific determinism laid the groundwork for the later secularization of fate.

A word of clarification is needed here. Some fatalists are so from the beginning of their awareness of the world. They do not evolve into fatalism. Others become fatalists, as is the case of some scientific determinists who developed into fatalists and felt they had no more need for faith in God. Still others keep their faith in God in a compartment away from their assumption of scientific determinism at their work.

The secularization of fate in the nineteenth and twentieth centuries had its peak in the work of Karl Marx (1818–83) and Friedrich Engels (1820–95). Marx ruled out any religious interpretation of the determined order of the universe and human life. He said: "The religious world is but the reflex of the real world. . . . The religious reflex of the real world can, in any case, only then finally vanish when the practical

relations of everyday life offer to man none but perfectly intelligible
and reasonable relations with regard to his fellow men and to nature."
His angle of vision is a historical determinism, a fate devoid of divine
governance. The social movement of peoples and economics is "a process of natural history, governed by laws independent of the human
will, consciousness, and intelligence." Friedrich Engels says in the
preface to *The Communist Manifesto:* "The whole history of mankind
(since the dissolution of primal tribal society holding land in common
ownership) has been a history of class struggles, contests between the
exploiting and the exploited, ruling and oppressed classes." He predicts
that the "oppressed class—the proletariat—cannot attain its emancipation from the sway of the exploiting and ruling class—the
bourgeoisie—without at the same time, and once and for all, emanci-
pating society at large from all exploitation, oppression, class distinc-
tions and class struggles."[10] For Marx and Engels, this emancipation
was the manifest destiny for communism and fate for capitalistic oppression.

We can, with the collapse of communism in Eastern Europe and the
Union of Soviet Socialist Republics, be prone to shrug off Marx and
Engels as museum pieces of history. However, the rampant cleavage of
our own country between the privileged and the underprivileged, the
sense of hopelessness that pervades the poverty-stricken and the well-
to-do prompts us to take seriously what Marx and Engels say about the
fatalism of class struggles. The life of churches and denominations is
being sorely strained by ideologies that remind us of the churches of
Germany in the 1930s in their response to the rise of Nazism.

In America today, church people tend to brush off as insignificant
the rise of neo-Nazism and the extremes of the far right that are actively
represented in television religious shows, candidacies for political
office, and efforts to control public institutions of education and government. Racism and anti-intellectualism, which seek a takeover of institutions of higher education and exhibit an intolerance of the realm
of public discourse, are very present. Rarely are they seen as fascistic
in their approach to life. This attitude was evident in Germany in the
1930s. Dietrich Bonhoeffer, the German Lutheran pastor who was finally executed by Hitler's soldiers, rebelled against the Lutheran church
leaders who went along with Hitler to get along.

Fate as secular and scientific determinism takes on a psychological
form in the thought of Sigmund Freud. Freud was a fatalist in his scientific determinism. He says: "The psychoanalyst is distinguished by an
especially strong belief in the determination of the psychic life. For him

there is nothing trifling, nothing arbitrary and lawless."[11] He recounts the story of *Oedipus Rex* in which Oedipus murders his father and unknowingly marries his mother and births two children by her.

Concerning this Freud says: "The *Oedipus Rex* is a tragedy of fate; its tragic effect depends on the all powerful will of the gods and the vain efforts of human beings threatened with disaster." He sees this set of causes and effects as the inevitable outworking of human nature. Even the trivial errors of family life are causally connected with the fateful emergence of deeper unconscious motives. Of the person who shrugs this interpretation off as merely "little accidents," he says, "Anyone thus breaking away from the determination of natural phenomenon, at any single point, has thrown out the scientific outlook on the world."[12] For Freud, human values come from our world of interactions with our parents. He rarely mentions human values arising from interaction with siblings. Human values are secular in origin, arising from the fate-filled human situation.

Contemporary psychological determinism finds an unerring fatalism in the impact of early childhood rearing upon the later personality disorders of adulthood. A maze of theories of family therapy postulate similar developmental determinism of present-day dysfunctions in the grown sons and daughters. At present, similar efforts are being made to explain dramatic exceptions to this developmental determinism. The "invulnerable child" or the "transcending child" are names given to children who become functional, creative, and reasonably happy adults in spite of destructive and dysfunctional families of origin. These persons demonstrate a hitherto unnoticed resilience to the threatening events and environment.[13]

William James very early challenged the fatalism of scientific determinism in words that are early anticipations of the concept of the invulnerable child who resists the drifts of a toxic environment. He questions the idea of determinism:

There is a *fatalistic* argument for determinism, however, which is radically vicious. When a man has let himself go time after time, he easily becomes impressed with the enormously preponderating influence of circumstances, heredity and habits, and temporary bodily dispositions, one over what might seem a spontaneity born for the occasion. "All is fate," he then says, "all is result of what preexists. . . . It is hopeless to resist the drift, vain to look for any new force coming in and less, perhaps, than anywhere else under the sun is there anything really mine in the decisions which I make." There is really no argument for simple determinism.[14]

The lucky are those who had the psychically perfect upbringing.

Then James makes a case for what he calls free effort, the opposite of a lucky fate:

> When a dreadful object is presented, or when life as a whole turns up its dark abysses to our view, then the worthless ones among us lose their hold on the situation altogether, and either escape from its difficulties by averting their attention, or if they cannot do that, collapse into yielding masses of plaintiveness and fear. . . . But the heroic mind does differently. To it, too, the objects are sinister and dreadful, unwelcome, incompatible with wished for things. But it can face them if necessary, without for that losing its hold upon the rest of life. The world thus finds in the heroic man its worthy match and mate; and the effort which he is able to put forth to hold himself erect and keep his heart unshaken is the direct measure of his worth and function in the game of life. He can *stand* the universe.[15]

Following the lead of both Freud and James, fatalism in scientific determinism is not a unanimous, agreed upon stance of scientists of today. However, the cumulative effect of those who espouse scientific determinism in a fatalistic way overpowers those who do not. The discovery of the DNA code in our physical constitutions, the interpretation of the effects of alcoholism as a familial disease, the long-term effects of sexual abuse of children by adults, the hereditary nature of schizophrenia and manic-depression and other illnesses have produced a quiet desperation and fatalism in the face of these disorders.

We can put a theological frame of meaning around these dark fates of humankind. The intelligence of a person is the candle of the Lord. The God and Father of our Lord Jesus Christ, the God of all comfort and the Father of mercies calls an intelligence consecrated to God and uses it to outwit, ameliorate, and provide a sense of mission in the face of these disabilities, losses, and terrifying episodes. This God—not just any God—suffers with us in the death, burial, and resurrection of Jesus Christ to bring light out of darkness, peace out of confusion, and a sense of purpose out of the suffering. The comfort with which God comforts becomes an instrument with which we comfort other people in any affliction. This assurance provides a meaning and purpose that fills us with hope and saves us from the despair of fatalism and the secular dependence on luck (see 2 Cor. 1:3–7).

Yet comfort does not happen magically or by chance of luck. As has been said before, the disciplines of patience producing endurance, endurance producing character, and character producing a hope that does not disappoint us must be the conscious, free efforts of a person.

He or she is enabled to do this by the power of the Holy Spirit, which pours the love of God into our hearts (see Rom. 5:1–5). The human strength derived from this discipline is courage.

Hans Kohut describes three empirical characteristics of such a person of courage, whom he calls a hero. These characteristics are clearly outside the realm of psychosis. The three features are these: "The presence of a fine sense of humor, the ability to respond to others with subtle empathy and . . . the suffusion of the personality with profound sense of peace and serenity—a mental state akin to wisdom."[16]

FATE AND THE WILL OF GOD

Fate has another interpretation for the believer in God—providence working out in a community. A very positive expression of providence is found in the dramatic story of Ruth. One reads: "She came and gleaned in the field behind the reapers. As it happened, she came to the part of the field belonging to Boaz" (Ruth 2:3). The "happening" is from the Hebrew word *miqreh,* meaning "chance" or "event." In the Elizabethan language of the King James Version, the word is translated "hap." Was it just a "happening," fortune, or luck that Ruth "just by chance" came to the part of the field belonging to Boaz? Or is there a deeper meaning in the unfolding events of her working with Boaz, being helped by him to get the best and the most grain in her gleaning, being chosen by him to become his wife, marrying him and giving birth to Obed, who became the grandfather of David, the king? Do these events, seen in retrospect, mean just what the finale of the story says: "The Lord made her conceive, and she bore a son." This child put her in direct lineage with King David and in the genealogy of Jesus Christ, the son of David, the son of Abraham (see Matt. 1:1–17). Of course, I put my faith in the providence of God in these events, both "seeing ahead" and "providing for" Ruth. Many would say that it was luck, a chance that turned out to make Ruth a fortunate woman. Theirs would be faith in luck.

Providence is seen in the destiny the Lord God had for Israel in delivering the Israelites out of slavery in Egypt. He commissioned Moses to say to Pharaoh: "Thus says the LORD: Israel is my firstborn son. I said to you, 'Let my son go that he may worship me'" (Exod. 4:22–23). This theme of the destiny of Israel is repeated in Exodus 7:3 and Deuteronomy 5:12–15, to name two of many such affirmations.

This same sense of the providence of God is apparent in Jeremiah's commission from the Lord to be a prophet: "Before I formed you in the womb I knew you, and before you were born I consecrated you; I appointed you a prophet to the nations" (Jer. 1:5). Jeremiah responded to the destiny of the Lord, but he became so discouraged that later he said: "Cursed be the day on which I was born! The day when my mother bore me, let it not be blessed! . . . Why did I come forth from the womb to see toil and sorrow, and spend my days in shame?" (Jer. 20:14, 18). Thus Jeremiah wrestled with the destiny that had been given to him.

Fate and Death

Jeremiah's complaint to God that he was ever born reflects the biblical stance toward death as one's fate. There is no biblical concept for fate, such as *moira* in the Greek religion or *Kismet* in Islam. To the contrary, in the Old and New Testaments one's death is in God's hands. Here life is God's gift. Life is to be lived, whereas death is to be left to God. For example, Moses, weary of trying to care for the Israelites in the wilderness, *asks* God to kill him (Num. 11:14–15). Elijah "went a day's journey into the wilderness, and . . . asked that he might die" (1 Kings 19:4). In both instances God answered by pointing them to a community of faith who could help bear their burdens. Moses was told to seek out seventy elders of Israel to "take some of the spirit that is on you and put it on them; and they shall bear the burden of the people along with you so that you will not bear it all by yourself" (Num. 11:17). God told Elijah that he should "anoint Elisha . . . in your place" and that God would have "seven thousand in Israel, all the knees that have not bowed to Baal, and every mouth that has not kissed him" (1 Kings 19:16, 18). God saw to it that in the midst of their despair they were not alone in their mission, and they were given strength for the living of their days.

More generally, death is seen as the universal plight of humankind. As Ecclesiastes asks: "How can the wise die just like fools?" (Eccl. 2:16b); and in 3:19: "For the fate of humans and the fate of animals is the same; as one dies, so dies the other." Also, Psalm 49:10, 12–13 says: "When we look at the wise, they die; fool and dolt perish together. . . . Mortals cannot abide in their pomp; they are like the animals that perish. Such is the fate of the foolhardy, the end of those who are pleased with their lot." This laconic wisdom about the fatefulness of death is echoed in Caesar's words in Shakespeare's *Julius Caesar* (Act II, Scene 2):

> Cowards die many times before their deaths; the valiant never taste
> of death but once. Of all the wonders that I yet have heard, it seems

to me most strange that men should fear; seeing that death, a necessary end, will come when it will come.

Theological Predestination

Fate as a secular belief has a whole new meaning in a spiritual
worldview. In the New Testament, fate takes on the character of predestination. It is brought to focus in God's action in Christ's salvation of
us and not upon our physical death. As the apostle Paul says in Romans
8:29: "For those whom he foreknew he also predestined to be conformed to the image of his Son." This predestination involves a vocation
or calling, not just a static transaction stamping those to be saved and
those to be damned. Paul continues: "And those whom he predestined
he also called; and those whom he called he also justified; and those
whom he justified he also glorified" (Rom. 8:30). The predestination,
calling, justification, and glorification come about through the believer's growing into conformity to the likeness of Christ in his suffering
and obedience even unto death.

This passage has been the battleground of interpreters throughout
Christian history. Augustine asserted that not only did God foreknow
our paths and actions, but God also willed that those he foreknew be
saved. Redemption is not in human merit but in God's own decree.

John Calvin is most often associated with predestination. He says,
"We shall never be persuaded as we ought that our salvation flows from
the free mercy of God as its fountain, until we are made acquainted
with his eternal election."[17]

If one looks at predestination from the angle of the vision of luck, it
would seem that those predestined for salvation were lucky and all others were unlucky. Calvin is attacked for his rigid determinism. Yet his
main concern was the security of the person in his or her salvation, the
assurance of God's love in Jesus Christ, and the sense of responsibility
as Christians that this confidence produces in genuine Christians.

Too often the discussions of predestination center upon the issue of
the lack of free will and election to the exclusion of Paul's emphasis
upon calling, vocation, and a sense of personal destiny. In so many
words he says, "and those whom he predestined he also called." God
called Abraham, who by faith went out not knowing where he went.
God called Jeremiah from his mother's womb. God called Paul to be
a light to the Gentiles. This sense of destiny resides in many people
today. To focus upon the calling brings the discussion of predestination out of the realm of abstraction into the practicalities of everyday
life.

CHRISTIAN FAITH AND FATALISM

We have explored some of the classical and contemporary tributaries of fatalism as a philosophy of life. An interpretive synthesis is now in order.

Fatalism interprets the universe, the relationship to God, and the human condition as a closed system. However, as Ludwig von Bertalanffy, the primary interpreter of systems, says: "Every *living* organism is essentially an open system. It maintains itself in a continuous inflow and outflow . . . so long as it is alive, in a state of chemical and thermodynamic equilibrium maintained in a so-called steady state."[18] This steady state is maintained by metabolism. He relates a closed system to inanimate existence, such as the motions of the planetary system. These are fixed and determined. The dependability of the universe rests upon its parts faithfully following their appointed works. Could it be that astrology is an attempt to bring stability to the flux and flow of the not-so-closed systems of living organisms? The open system of the human being is changed by the inflow of information and the resulting feedback from the information received.

The Christian faith differs from secular fatalism in that we as living organisms are not the subjects of fatalism or closed systems. We maintain stability through a balanced homeostasis of our whole organism. We grow and develop through the input of information that creates a change as we respond to it. In fatalism, this happens by chance. In the Christian faith, divine providence cares for us in this way.

Nevertheless, there are fixed constants even in the open systems of our lives. The two most momentous constants are our birth and our death. These are the "common lot" of all human beings. Around them can cluster most of our fatalistic feelings of good and bad luck. But as Christians, our sense is that we are in God's care; as the apostle Paul says, God "allotted the times of [our] existence and the boundaries of the places where [we] would live" (Acts 17:26).

Between the set boundaries of birth and death, life is an open system fed and nourished by God-given information. It is not dependent on feckless luck, nor upon having a "break." We can capitulate to addictions or to nonfunctional personality disorders. We can live by fate and say: "This is the way I am. All my family is or was this way. Why can't you accept me as I am?" This is a practical fatalism, although it need not be so. The biblical concept for this is hardness of heart or unteachableness of the kind that Pharaoh exhibited and of which Jesus spoke when referring to Moses' reason for granting a writ of divorcement.

The Spirit of God can open our minds to the wisdom of God to change our minds.

Neither the universe nor our persons nor our families nor the communities we live in are closed, fated systems. Elements of free effort fueled by adequate information are available to us if we are not too hardheaded to learn or too fearful to respond with courage. Even so, the universe and our persons are subject to chance and accident. The next chapter takes the discussion of luck into this arena.

4. Chance

*I*n a fatalist's world, whatever happens is accepted as inevitable. If persons feel that their destiny gives them courage to take an active role in responding to the events of life, they will tend to say that they have good fortune. However, if persons feel cursed with one experience of bad luck after another, they will say that they are fated to a continuous stream of bad luck.

Others, however, view the world as a world of chance happenings that may be either good or bad, without any pattern or meaning. If they consider themselves lucky, they will be eager to take chances in the face of an unknown outcome. If they consider themselves unlucky and as having never won in taking chances, they will be supercautious in what they perceive as a hostile world.

Therefore, our next step in examining luck as secular faith is to consider the role and function of chance in the lives of lucky and unlucky people.

THE MEANING OF CHANCE

Fatalism leaves little or no room for the fortuitous happenings that we call chance. The word "chance" has a long history. It reaches back to the Latin word *cadentia,* meaning a falling, especially the falling of dice. It also means fortune, good or bad. In the modern use, chance means whatever happens—events that come randomly and unpredictably, without any apparent cause.

Chance has two dimensions. First, chance can be thought of as an absolutely fortuitous happening, spontaneous, and without cause or any particular meaning. Thus chance is wrapped in mystery in a mysterious universe and in the sphere of people's relations to each other. Second, others relate chance and coincidence. The concurrence of two events seems to produce some meaning or result. Some religious people take these coincidences as signs from God. People who are aware of no divine presence will believe that these coincidences are just either good luck or bad luck.

Chance as Coincidence

Plato described causation and chance in terms of the automatic activity of the human eye being acted upon by light or the absence of light:

> The lover of intellect and knowledge ought to explore causes of intelligent nature [such as the light], and, secondly, those . . . being moved by others [such as the eyes]. . . . Both kinds of causes should be acknowledged by us, but a distinction should be made between those endowed with mind and are the workers of things fair and good, *and those which are deprived of intelligence and produce changes effective without order or design* (italics mine).[1]

A homely example from today's American life exemplifies Plato's distinction between things that are guided by intelligence and those that are without intelligence and therefore are guided by matters of chance. Neither a wagon nor an automobile has intelligence to direct its course. The driver of either a horse-drawn wagon or an automobile supplies the intelligence to guide the vehicle and reduce the chances of an accident. However, in the case of a horse-drawn carriage, there is also present the intelligence of the horse. If the driver falls asleep or is drunk, the intelligence of the horse will, one hopes, enable it to avoid other vehicles and find the way home. Thus the dangers of chance are minimized. However, the direction of the automobile is subject only to the intelligence of the driver. If the driver falls asleep or is drunk, the chances of an accident are exponentially higher. The chances taken by a drunken driver account for twenty-one thousand deaths by accident. The absence of intelligence can have lethal results.

As Augustine says, "The force of chance is diffused throughout the whole order of things."[2] Plato identifies intelligence as the vital force enabling a person to navigate the flow and ebb of events in his or her life, stamping order, meaning, and wisdom in the chancy circumstances of life. We use our intelligence to link seemingly coincidental events into a cause-and-effect sequence. For example, does cancer just happen, or can research identify causes and prevent it? Many carcinogens have been identified. However, why does a person who does not smoke, drink, eat carcinogenic foods, or have a family history of cancer come down with cancer—first in the colon, then in the liver, and then in the lungs? Is this mere chance? Does this just happen? Is it a mere coincidence? Here the attempt to undertake an intelligent tracking of cause fades out into mystery.

Aristotle discusses chance and spontaneity in his work *Physics.* He attempts to classify explanations of events in the universe. He describes chance as "the indefinite law . . . inscrutable to man." He uses analogies from human relations.[3] However, in modern physics the element of fortuitous and spontaneous events is also discussed. Werner Heisenberg in 1927 introduced the principle of uncertainty (or indeterminacy) which "held that it is impossible to determine at the same time both the position and velocity of an electron."[4] Observation disturbs the particular system so that the result or outcome is always uncertain. Even at the level of the atom, the elements of chance and spontaneity are present.[5]

The most important issues in this technical discussion of chance and spontaneity or fortuitousness are the issue of mystery and the issue of uncertainty. In a world of chance and mysteriously spontaneous events, the spiritual reality of anxiety about the unknown grips the heart and imagination of a person. In the face of spontaneous events, the sense of awe and wonder captures the mind and heart as well.

Chance and Miracles

The random, unpatterned, unrepeatable chance or coincidence is considered good luck or bad luck depending upon its consequences for those to whom it happened. If what happens is, for example, a spontaneous remission of a serious disease, some people attribute it to luck and consider themselves fortunate. Other people who depend upon the providence of God consider the spontaneous recovery a miracle. Likewise, a spontaneous calamity may be interpreted as the punishment of God.

The major difference between a miracle and a mere random event is that a miracle is said by the believer to have an unobservable, mysterious cause—namely, God. The random event is purely spontaneous and fortuitous. Furthermore, a miracle ceases to be a miracle if it can be reproduced again and again. Similarly, a chance occurrence that can be reproduced ceases to be a chance occurrence. In both instances, when a cause has been discovered, both the miraculous and the spontaneity are dissolved in predictablity. At the least, a pattern or design of such events has been discerned. The devoutly religious person may see the discovery of ways to repeat the miracle as a form of revelation of God's wisdom about the universe. A miracle is understood as the operation of unknown laws. The secular-minded person may believe that the discovery is good luck. As Colin Brown says:

Depending upon their perspective, one person might interpret the event as fortuitous, another as a stroke of luck, and yet another as an expression of the grace of God. In each case the experience is the same. But the meaning attached to it depends in part on the frame of reference that is brought to the interpretation.[6]

As a result of these differing frames of reference, I have chosen to call luck a secular faith because it is a secular hermeneutic of events that from a religious point of view may be seen as acts of the providence of God. A persistent theme of the Old and New Testaments is that of deliverance. A fortuitous event happens that delivers a person from evil and/or destruction and death. For example, Psalm 116:8 says, "For you have delivered my soul from death, my eyes from tears, my feet from stumbling."

Behavioral scientists readily recognize spontaneous recoveries. They will often celebrate a miracle with the devoutly religious person who interprets the recovery as a miracle. Yet scientists insist on trying to reproduce that which to them is first a chance happening. Nevertheless, ecclesiastical authorities insist that if a spontaneous event can be reproduced it cannot be considered a miracle. Rather, it is a work of human beings. By such a standard, for example, the discovery of the polio vaccine by Salk would not be a miracle. Yet it is, in my interpretation, a revelation from God as well as a discovery by Salk. The struggles to unravel the mystery of the AIDS virus represent the dedicated efforts of scientists on one side of the mystery and God on the other side of the mystery struggling to meet each other. If the discovery comes about "by chance," it will be no less a miracle by reason of the fact that it can be reproduced again and again.

William G. Pollard says, "The context of providence is history which happens only once."[7] However, if a chance happening occurs that is disastrous in its results, we usually do not call it a miracle, because we attribute only good happenings to the miraculous work of God. In our attempt to find meaning in the unhappy event, we have two other choices or frames of reference by which to interpret it. We can engage in theodicy; that is, we attempt to explain why with a good God "bad things happen to good people," to use Rabbi Harold Kushner's title, or second, we attribute our misfortune to our own sin for which God has punished us, or to the devil who has in this happening thwarted temporarily the providence of God. A more realistic faith in God in Jesus Christ reminds us: "I have said this to you, so that in me you may have peace. In the world you face persecution. But take courage; I have conquered the world!" (John 16:33). Indeed, as Carl Sandburg once commented, "Souls are made of endurance."

CHANCE AND MAKING YOUR LUCK

Chance, then, is wrapped in mystery and uncertainty. In such a world of chance, we are often gripped by the anxiety of the unknown. The fear of the unknown is one of the most profound, universal fears that we have. However, not only are we gripped by fear, but we are also fascinated, and our sense of cleverness is activated by the mystery. Anxiety, fascination, and cleverness take different people in different directions.

Some people interpret a chance happening as good or bad luck. They fix their faith on a secular belief in luck. An example of this is Willie Shoemaker, the world-renowned jockey. He was totally paralyzed by an automobile accident. He can operate a wheelchair by inhaling and exhaling through a tube. He observes his race horses and gives his trainers instructions about caring for them. In a television tribute to Shoemaker, his wife was asked how she felt about their new situation in life. She replied: "We have been dealt a hand of cards. We choose to play the hand rather than to turn it in." This is their manifesto about the future. They will take the situation that bad luck has dealt them and use their determination, cleverness, and perseverance to outwit their ill fortune.

Others may attempt to avoid responsibility by attributing to chance something that has very clear causes. In the spring of 1992, the House of Representatives was rocked by the scandal of bouncing checks in the House bank. A Kentucky representative at the outset denied having any such checks on his record. Then the complete list was published. He had 152 checks on the list. In addition to this, he became implicated in the mammoth savings and loan scandal that cost the taxpayers over five hundred billion dollars. In his spring primary he was resoundingly defeated. Some would say that he had run out of luck. A more reflective assessment would be that he had been substituting luck for integrity for some time.

Many people trust in luck to substitute for the discipline needed to cause their dreams to come to pass. They fantasize about the time when they will get their "big break." In the meantime they trust in luck to bring this big break into reality. In Chapter 1 mention was made of some children whose parents are successful. The parents denied themselves of luxuries, were extremely thrifty, and took advantage of every opportunity that came their way. They worked hard and applied intelligence to every task, developing skill as they went. They became affluent and were able to see to it that their son did not have as difficult a life as they had experienced.

Now the son is trusting luck to bring his fantasy into reality. He has carefully avoided the factors of discipline, hard work, and intentionally developed skill. His "big break" will take care of everything in one fell swoop of luck. Luck takes the place of personal commitment, preparation, routine, method, practice, and the honing of skills. He leaves those unpleasant chores to his parents. He dreams of being an artist, a musician, or a business entrepreneur without being willing to do what is needed to fulfill his dream. He is counting on luck with a fervent faith.

In contrast, other people recognize the need to take control of events. Recently I went to my dentist to have a gold crown crafted for a seventy-four year old tooth. He shaped the tooth with his drill and then took an impression by which the crown would be made. When I returned to him three weeks later, he took the crown in his hand and said, "I wonder if this thing is going to fit." He dropped it in place, and it fitted perfectly. He was elated. "It is an exact fit! All I have to do is cement it in place."

I asked him, "Was that chance, coincidence, luck, or providence?" He paused for a moment and said, "How about skill?" I said, "I think it was skill! Congratulations!"

Long years of discipline had gone into his developing the skill to produce such results. He had not taken any shortcuts. He had learned by instruction, practice, and effort how to produce such results. He had not trusted chance, coincidence, luck, or even providence. Hard work and care for detail had produced the skill to accomplish such precision. Good luck is a lazy person's estimate of the hard worker's success.

The story of a billionaire who got his start with a dime store in a small Arkansas town and at the time of his death was the nation's most successful discount retailer enchants many of us. Many would say that he was lucky. It would be more accurate to say that he was intelligent and diligent. He made his own good luck. Conversely, those who did not use the intelligence they had been given nor apply the diligence required by each given opportunity were the makers of their own bad luck.

The technological revolution has created a world in which technological skill is a necessity for even survival, to say nothing of becoming a brilliant success. At the same time, the mass educational system, described by David Elkind as "factory education," is turning out graduates who cannot read, know little mathematics, and have few if any skills. The fortunate, or lucky, persons will be those who happen to get a dedicated teacher who singles them out of the crowd and inspires them to believe in their gifts and to submit themselves to the disciplines that result in their becoming incredibly skilled persons. Then these persons will tend to see themselves, not as lucky persons, but as grateful persons to have had such teachers.

The person with an intelligence dedicated to God and filled with respect for the mystery of the universe uses that intelligence to exercise carefulness and care in a world of chance. The careful person assesses the chances even when causes are unknown. Events for which there is no known cause could be either random events or part of an unknown pattern or sequence. Random events alone may be inexplicable to intelligent observation, but patterned happenings can be tracked and elements of predictability established. For example, the reason for many medications' efficacy in healing may not be known. However, in noting the pattern of events in recovering patients in double-blind drug trials, physicians can establish the usefulness of a given medication even though the reasons why it is helpful are yet to be discovered. For example, the value of electroconvulsive therapy for depression was discovered when patients with seizures were observed becoming clear of depression after a seizure. Several chemical means of inducing seizures were tried and discarded because of severe side effects. Then researchers found that the use of very small amounts of electrical stimulation of the brain brought effective relief from depression. The exact explanation of why this happens is still hypothetical. However, this demonstrates how coincidences can be observed to fall into a pattern that can be reproduced.

The element of chance can be brought under a measure of control, utility, and predictability. Hence, care and carefulness are productive in the face of chance. Coincidences can be catalogued and patterns recognized. Such observations provide positive or negative feedback. The individual person can develop a code of behavior to make the chances work to his or her safety and/or favor rather than to his or her danger and/or disfavor. These findings can be taught to children and less experienced persons to aid them. This teaching of a code of carefulness calls for care on the part of the teacher and the persons taught. This is epitomized in our farewell greetings of each other, such as, "Take care!" or "Drive carefully!"

Not observing these rituals of carefulness and care leads to blind dependence upon luck, summed up in the description of a person as "happy go lucky" in one's way of life. On the other hand, carefulness can become obsessiveness, a character trait that is useful in airline pilots, train engineers, surgeons, and the like. It can have its painful expression in the fear-driven illness of the compulsive obsessive personalities who check and recheck door locks, electric outlets, and the arrangement of bedcovers before they can go to sleep at night. Taken to such an extreme, the element of carefulness and "taking no chances" snuffs out the freedom and spontaneity of life.

CHANCE AND THE HUMAN SITUATION

To be human is to face constantly the unpredictable and seemingly spontaneous events of human existence. Life is full of surprises. Consequently, the human being is by nature an anxious being. As Rollo May says:

> The alert citizen, we may assume, would be aware not only of the more obvious anxiety creating situations in our day, such as threats of war, of the uncontrolled atom bomb, and of radical political or economic upheaval; but also of the less obvious anxiety in himself as well as in his fellow man—namely the inner confusions, psychological disorientation, and uncertainty with respect to values and acceptable standards of conflict. Hence, to endeavor to "prove" the pervasiveness of anxiety in our days is as unnecessary as the proverbial carrying coals to Newcastle.[8]

Several dimensions of this universal human condition make the generalization specific and to the point.

Child Birthing and Rearing

Jesus likened his death, burial, and resurrection to the travail of a woman in childbirth. "When a woman is in labor, she has pain, because her hour has come. But when her child is born, she no longer remembers the anguish because of the joy of having brought a human being into the world" (John 16:21). However, this joy is followed by a pilgrimage of anxiety even when the child is born healthy and well-formed. Moreover, the chances that the child will not be healthy and well-formed are exponentially higher today because of the too common use by parents of drugs, alcohol, and tobacco, and because of the increased pollution in the atmosphere.

Even if the child comes to birth as a hale and hearty youngster, the anguish of parenthood lies in considering the chances of disease, accident, and behavioral disorders in the child's growth. Archibald MacLeish, in *J.B.*, his modern version of the story of Job, says that a father "fixes his hopes on little children"; then that a fever "or a running dog can kill between dark and day."[9] For example, parents are concerned about sudden infant death syndrome, when for a seemingly indefinite cause a child dies in its crib while asleep.

Beyond the anxieties that parents experience during their child's infancy, they must contend with what is the essence of growing up for a child—experimenting with new objects and activities. Parents exercise a tightrope walk in letting the child adventure, explore, and learn for himself or herself, or in keeping tight control to eliminate all chances of harm. This tension rises to an all-time crescendo in the adolescent years when the dangers of pregnancy, drug overdose, alcoholism, and auto accidents are at every hand as the growing young person faces temptation and opportunity. With the advent of AIDS in our sexually promiscuous world, the dangers are multiplied. Also, each generation in this century has been confronted by a war—World War I, World War II, the Korean War, the Vietnam War, and Desert Storm. These wars are engineered by older people, but they are largely carried out by persons who are eighteen to twenty-five years of age. These sons and daughters are put into high risk, chancy situations. Parents are anxious about them *all* the time, whereas the young person may feel danger only periodically and be having a relatively good time the rest of the while. In all these ways and more, the experience of child bearing and child rearing is a perpetual pilgrimage of coping with chance.

Chance and Economic Uncertainty

Some have said that chances in the economic realm are "opportunities." For example, persons trying to enter the workforce are looking for a chance to prove their worth as workers. They may do all of the expected things—prepare résumés, ask for interviews, present themselves well—and wait, wait, wait. College graduates often blandly assume that a degree grants them a good job. It does not. They keep hoping for a chance, an opportunity. They say no one will "give them a break." (This phrase might come from a break in pool or billiards "where once a player breaks the racked balls he or she has a chance to make a long successful run."[10])

Energetic entrepreneurs tend to make their own chances or breaks in life. They go through a starvation period of prudent poverty and discipline themselves for a self-chosen task. Caution and persistence are their trademarks. However, passive-dependent and passive-aggressive persons tend to depend quite heavily on spontaneous chance to bring them their big break in life. They are likely to project the blame for their bad luck on the people around them who do not appreciate them for their real worth. However, they let time pass aimlessly by without taking initiative to shape their own destinies.

Quite apart from these two extremes of actively seeking an opportunity and passively waiting for something to happen, a break or an opportunity in life is a very real and palpable need. Whole underclasses of people live their lives in quiet desperation, with nothing, as Robert Frost says, "to look back upon with pride or to look forward to with hope."[11] Their predicament points to the need for persons who are mentors to younger people who are committed to creating chances, opportunities, or breaks in their behalf. The stewardship of influence is rarely thought of in the whole sphere of chance, but the reality that one person can give another a chance, maybe even a second or third chance, is a part of the stuff of which life is made.

Chance and the Desire
for Instant Gratification

Chance, spontaneous happenings, and opportunity have built-in time clocks of gestation. Yet the pandemic desire for instant gratification of desires prompts people to ignore these built-in time clocks. An egg, with time, can hatch into a chicken. With much less time, it can be immediate gratification for a hungry appetite. Much more complex is the feverish quest for sexual and romantic happiness. Great chances may be taken, ignoring the admonition from the Book of Common Prayer that the relationship of a man and woman not be "entered into unadvisedly, or lightly, but reverently, discreetly, advisedly, and in the fear of God."

The desire for immediate gratification causes chances in human relations to rise exponentially. The calculation of hazard is too often forgotten in the pell-mell frenzy for gratification. The stress of the immediate satisfaction of desires cuts short the time of reflection in decision making. Weighing and considering are nullified. The element of chance is at an all-time high in the life of the individual person who assumes himself or herself to be unique and special. Such a person feels entitled to whatever he or she wants at the moment the desire hits. The narcissism of the person spawns this self-perception.

Human beings as a species are enthralled by a cluster of illusions. We make up the difference between our illusion and the realm of reality with our secular faith in luck. We act on these illusions, assuming that we will be lucky; we try to sneak by the grim chances that we are taking. Neither sober caution nor spiritual codes of faith protect us. We rest on our luck. We put our faith in luck as we run the gauntlet of chance.

Illusions are very evident in the present crisis of the spread of AIDS.[12] On November 8, 1991, Magic Johnson, the superlative basketball player, shook America to a rude awakening when he announced that he was HIV-positive, a state inevitably followed by the disease of AIDS. This disease has a 100 percent fatality rate, and there is no known cause or cure for it. The risk of getting it can be reduced dramatically by avoiding promiscuous sexual behavior. The danger of contracting the disease is a medical call for mutual fidelity between two uninfected partners in any form of sexual activity.

The risk can also be reduced by avoiding the sharing of dirty needles in illicit drug use. In some cases, the disease is also contracted through blood transfusions. The disease cannot be contracted in the common routines of a household if there is no exchange of body fluids. Between 1981 and 1991, over a million persons have been infected, and 126,159 have died. (Remarkably enough, in the same span of time as many as 200,000 persons have died in alcohol-related car accidents!)

This disease, and especially Magic Johnson's dramatic announcement, has called nationwide attention to the way people take chances. The facts about these chances have been widely published in media documentaries and in school and church education groups. The Surgeon General of the United States placed these data in every mailbox in the country, yet people continue to take chances.

The illusions that underlie such blatant risk-taking portray the way a secular faith in luck pushes people into the hazards of a known threat of death. Three such illusions are characteristic of most if not all of us as human beings.

Illusion One: Every human being unconsciously believes that neither he nor she nor his or her loved ones will die. The threat of death from AIDS, automobile or airplane accidents, and lung cancer from smoking, for example, is selectively ignored because of this illusion. A person who smokes three packs of cigarettes a day will say, "Everybody has to die sometime; this doesn't worry me." Yet this luck-inspired defense assumes that death will come in an instant. However, emphysema and/or lung cancer may gradually asphyxiate the person over a long period of years. Essentially, such people unconsciously believe they will not die. A person driven by sexual desires does not think, much less believe, that his or her fate could be to contract the virus that will lead to AIDS, which will ultimately kill.

Illusion Two: Unconsciously, people tend to believe that they can do anything they want to do. Nothing limits their freedom to do as they please. The reality of the limits of their situation as creatures of God does not temper their assumptions about the possibilities in life. Today in the current "me" generation, this illusion is more rampant than in previous, more austere eras, such as during the scourge of syphilis before the 1940s. Since the sexual revolution of the 1960s, this illusion is in full force in the sexual behavior of people. Not even the grim facts about AIDS deter them from this childish illusion of omnipotence.

This illusion also was whispered into the ear of Eve by the serpent: "For God knows that when you eat of it your eyes will be opened, and you will be like God, knowing good and evil" (Gen. 3:5). Erich Fromm says of this: "The Biblical text does not even mention the word 'sin.' Man challenges the supreme power of God, and he is able to challenge it because he is potentially God. . . . [H]is first act of disobedience . . . is the beginning of human freedom."[13] The illusion, however, is that human freedom is unlimited. We do not think that we are *as* gods. We think we *are* gods. The elements of chance cannot touch us. As gods, the fickle finger of misfortune, bad luck, wrongly taken chances cannot touch us. To assume that we are "as god" is the parent temptation/sin.

Another form of the illusion that we can do anything we choose is that there are no limits to our powers of control; we are and must be perfect. We delude ourselves that everything must be fail-safed by *us.* This leads us into the blind alley of compulsive obsessional behavior. All chance must be ruled out. Life must be perfectly predictable. If it is not, we are failures, defeated. Our imperfection rises up to haunt us. Rollo May gently pulls us back to our basic humanness and asks for the "courage of imperfection." He even speaks of our having the "ability to fail." Perfectionism consigns us to the "minor battlefields" of life. It keeps us from getting out of our "own little backyards" where the chance of failure is at a minimum.[14]

Illusion Three: Human beings as individuals and peer groups consider ourselves as exceptions to all the thousand mortal ills to which the flesh is heir. We suffer the same temptation to which Jesus was tempted by the devil: "Jump from this temple and you will not be injured in any way" (see Luke 4:9–11). The law of gravity does not apply to you! You are an exception! Yet Jesus knew that he was not an exception. His humanity was complete. He resisted the illusion of the temptation and refused to make an exception of himself.

Even in the face of the facts about AIDS as a killer disease with a 100 percent mortality rate, people ignore the facts because, they say, "It may happen to other people, but it won't happen to me." They leave off the rest of the illusion: "I am an exception!"

These illusions not only lead into taking a chance on AIDS. They underlie other defective decisions in life as well. These defective decisions are generated by an inarticulate but vitally active faith in luck.

They relieve the people of personal responsibility for a reality-based disciplined life. Life is lived in the same world of chance. Such a life calls for a sober refusal to live under these illusions and wholehearted commitment to a faith that will not shrink from the realities of a risky existence in a real world of chances. Thus we do not live under any illusion that we are never going to die, that we can do anything we choose, and that we are an exception to the laws of the universe. Instead, we gather all the information available, calculate our chances, and act with wisdom and caution. Faith in God, not luck, illumines such wisdom. If we are living under illusions, we need to submit ourselves to the discipline of disillusioning ourselves before life does it for us. The apostle Paul reminds us: "So then let us not fall asleep [in our illusions] as others do, but let us keep awake and be sober . . . since we belong to the day . . . and put on the breastplate of faith and love, and for a helmet the hope of salvation" (1 Thess. 5:6–8).

CHANCE AND FAITH

Søren Kierkegaard helps us understand more fully the tensions within us as we are called upon to make decisions in which broad chances are being taken, luck trusted, and confusion encountered. Kierkegaard identifies three such polarities, or tensions, in the human self.

First, the tension between *finitude and infinitude* calls for a synthesis, or balance, in our being. "The self is the conscious synthesis of finitude which relates itself to itself, a task to become itself, a task which can be performed only by means of a relationship to God." Only God is infinite. We are finite. We cannot gauge our finitude by comparing ourselves with ourselves or other finite human beings (see 2 Cor. 10:12). The presence of God makes this vivid, clear, and decisive. Joseph asked his brothers, "Am I in the place of God?" (Gen. 50:19). If he considered himself only in relation to them, he would never have known his true place in life. In relation to God, it was unmistakable as to what his place was. This tension is very akin to our illusion that we can do everything and there are no limits to our powers.[15]

Second, the tension between *possibility and necessity* is always with the self before God. "For God all things are possible," says Kierkegaard. But we are brought to our utmost extremity when *no* possibility exists. We are trapped in total necessity. There are *no* chances. However, "if God's will is only the necessary, man is essentially as speechless as the mutes."[16] The opening of many possibilities of life tempts us to ignore the necessities and clearly picture the person who has all the chances possible and can bypass the negative possibilities of bad luck, the fell clutch of circumstances. As Kierkegaard says, we can become intoxicated on infinity and possibility.

Third, we live between the antithesis of being *conscious and unconscious.* Awareness puts us in control of our actions, unconsciousness puts us out of control. "Clearness is requisite about oneself." Opposite to this is "complete mystification." Clarity is imperative when we hazard closeness and trust our luck in mystification. As Kierkegaard says, "man prefers to dwell in the cellar, that is, sensuousness" to living in the spirit-driven area of consciousness of being a responsible self.[17] There one takes chances, runs risks, and makes faulty decisions.

These three polarities illumine the nature of human nature in our world of chance.

Chance Taking and
the Community of Faith

Our community of faith is a fellowship of believers—not in luck—but in Christ and in each other. A community of faith may be and often is an intimate segment of a church. The larger fellowship of the church provides a body of beliefs, a pattern of spiritual rituals, and a clear identity for the smaller cells of communities of faith that form clusters within its membership. However, the small clusters are made up of people who know each other well, participate in each other's times of celebration of good fortune, and commiserate with each other during times of ill fortune. They dwell together in the realistic awareness that their lives are made up of a series of chance events, risky encounters, and hazardous possibilities of life. No blind faith in luck covers these events. To the contrary, the brunt of chance circumstances is taken as part of the stuff of which life is made. Life is seen as both good and rewarding and as unfair and unlucky. These ambiguous events are put into the larger context of two fundamental functions of faith in God. First, the God and Father of our Lord Jesus Christ is "the Father of mercies and the God of all comfort." Second, life as we live it is afflicted with sufferings, bad luck, hazardous chances, and all manner of human suffering. The Father of mercies and the God of all comfort does not cause or originate these sufferings. To the contrary, God—not just any god—comforts us in all our afflictions. God's purpose in doing this is to enable us to become a comfort to each other in times of bad luck, sad fortune, and affliction (see 2 Cor. 1:3–7).

This kind of caring community can arise out of its suffering, whether it is focused upon God or not. Combat soldiers are welded into a family of hazard, chance, or luck in the harm's way of battle. In a research report on combat stress during World War II, Roy Grinker, M.D., and John Spiegel say:

> Some of the men expect [the flight surgeon] to be a kindly father, others, a friendly brother. . . . [S]ome will want mothering and comforting while yet others will expect scolding and punishing. . . . However, almost always, studies of returnees reveal that [a] lost comrade has been identified with a brother or father figure. . . . The relationship to the brothers of the group was one of extreme altruism and everything was share and share alike.[18]

Thus the community of faith is born in a world of chance. We become sons and daughters of encouragement to each other. We "put heart" into each other. No one has to run the gauntlet of fiery chance alone. We are bound to each other with bonds of affection and steadfast commitment. We live a life of hard realism and not illusion about the chanciness of the world of which we are a part. We do not sleep or delude ourselves about our common participation in the world of chance. We see the chances of life steadily and do not blink or live in a realm of illusion. When ill fortune, bad luck, or a bad chance overcomes us, we look on this as a part of the fabric of human life and a result of the freedom God has given us.

The Protective Function of the Church

Chance is in the hinterland of the consciousness of people of the church in the framing of their taboos, beliefs, and practices. The church is often criticized for being so conservative, cautious, and protective of its membership. Even if we grant that this attitude stifles and inhibits some people, we must be realistic and admit that the church is at least not leaving the well-being of its members to chance nor operating on luck as a form of faith. The taboos against the use of alcohol and the practices of recreational and promiscuous sex would not be there if there were no ill chances, bad luck, or severe danger inherent in them. One could find fault that these taboos do not extend to the chances involved in smoking, in the use of food in excess, and in the irresponsible use of automobiles. The Seventh Day Adventists, for example, have gone far in avoiding the chances associated with the exposure to toxic substances such as carcinogens. However, not even they have sought through teaching and example to emphasize the safe use of automobiles. They, along with other communities of faith, leave this to chance and luck.

Thus luck and chance, even in the most cautious communities of faith, exist as a "secular faith" alongside the forthrightly religious discipline of the fellowship of faith.

5. Probability

*B*elievers in luck fall into one of at least two large categories. First, there are those who believe in absolute, unqualified luck and have a blind faith in luck. For them things "just happen." If what happens is in the person's favor, it is good luck. If what happens is adversity, it is bad luck. These persons evaluate luck in terms of their own self-interest.

Second, there are those who believe in luck only to a certain extent. They make every attempt to determine the degree of probability that a given happening will or will not come to pass. Then they build their pattern of behavior on that probability. They go even further and identify the particular factors that will improve or weaken the probabilities. They believe that if they can know the numerous factors that cause a certain event to come to pass, then they can control those factors and change or prevent the event. They thus try to take luck out of the realm of probability and make a certainty of it.

Once I was on a panel along with a Jewish rabbi, a clinical psychologist, a psychiatrist, and a clinical social worker. The clinical psychologist asked me, "If we come to that point at which we can know all the variables in human diseases and are able to control them to prevent human disease, what would be your thought as to the necessity of believing in God?" I responded: "When that time comes, my friend, the rabbi would have to change his theology from waiting for the Messiah to admitting that you, the Messiah, had come. Your hope that you will be able to manage and control randomness or luck is a kind of faith in itself."

This second kind of belief in luck is the confidence that probability can be reduced or eliminated by removing the factors that contribute to the possibility that an adverse event will happen. The hope of the clinical psychologist is a very necessary one for research to continue. However, the way he stated his belief indicated that he had a secular faith in his own power to manipulate and control reality, to master the randomness of experience. Luck is evident when many discoveries are accidental results of the search for the solution of some other problem.

Or they may be the side effects, let us say, of a heart medication or a painkiller.

This chapter is devoted to a discussion of probability; that is, calculating the potential for the *kind* of luck a person may anticipate.

THE MEANING OF PROBABILITY

The words "probability" and "probable" come from the Latin word *probare* (verb form), meaning to test, to approve, or to prove. In its adjective form, the Latin word is *probabilis*, meaning probable, credible, not impossible. The English word "probable" means to have more evidence for than against, or, supported by evidence strong enough that one can logically assume that a certain thing may or will or will not happen. Probability means that one has reasonable ground for presuming that a thing either has happened or is likely to happen. It also involves weighing the logical consequences of all the available evidence. It is based upon careful observation of events. The observer draws conclusions about what outcomes can be expected when certain conditions are present.

Probability was a concern of Galileo (1564–1642) who, in addition to being an astronomer and physicist, was an expert on the game of dice. He once advised an Italian nobleman who was an avid gambler that it would be wiser for him to bet on 10 coming up on the dice more often than 9. Galileo had found through his research that 10 would win 51.92 percent of the time compared with 48.08 percent for the 9. In addition to advising his patron about the road to riches, Galileo was working out some of the first probability theories.[1]

A French mathematician, Pierre-Simon Laplace, finally formulated the theory of probability regarding a set of events or happenings. In a set of events, a number of likely outcomes are probable. The probability factor of the number of desired outcomes in relation to the total possible results forms the *ratio* of probabilities. For example, in the tossing of a coin, assuming a coin with heads and tails, the probability of heads turning up has a ratio of 1 out of 2, or 1/2. No matter how many times the coin is tossed, this ratio of 1/2 is constant.

Another example of probability is calculating the possibility of drawing an ace and king in order from a suit (13) of cards that have been shuffled. The chances of drawing an ace would be 1 in 13; then the chances of drawing a king from the remaining twelve cards would be 1 in 12. However, the chance of drawing the ace and king in order would be 1/12 multiplied by 1/13 or 1 in 156 times. An amusing example of application of probability theory is the "birthday problem." If there are twenty-four people at a party, what is the probability of any two of them having the same birthday? (For the sake of simplicity, assume that anyone born on February 29 has February 28 as his or her birthday.) "Contrary to intuition, the probability is slightly larger than 1/2 and rises rapidly if the number (at the party) is increased."[2] Such an outcome may not seem credible, but it can be tested by making a game of it at a party or in a classroom.

THE USES OF PROBABILITY

The principles behind the theory of probability are developed and applied in a highly complex way in statistical work. On the basis of highly sophisticated use of mathematics, the probabilities of outcomes are estimated. They are applied in innumerable areas of human endeavor such as bridge building, automobile safety, merchandising, political opinion polling as to which candidate is preferred, and moral decision making between two or more "goods" or two or more evils. In medicine, predicting the chances, or outcome, of particular treatment modalities is important in determining what treatment is to be used for particular diseases. The interweaving of faith with luck regarding each of these can be made clear.

Probability and Medical Conditions

Calculating the probabilities that a person will recover, become more disabled, or die is one the most serious examples of the use of probability theory. Here the stakes are high. The issues of determining the probability of good or bad luck are often matters of life or death.

Robert D. Trugg, M.D., and Allen S. Brett, M.D., of Harvard Medical School, and Joel Frader, M.D., of the University of Pittsburgh have pinpointed the several medical conditions in which there is almost certain absence of any probability that the patient will live.

The first condition is maintaining terminally ill patients on mechanical life support systems indefinitely. For example, an eighty-six-year-old woman has been on a mechanical ventilator for more than a year. Her husband is a very religious man who insists on keeping her on the ventilator. He insists that dying is in God's hands and not those of human beings. An attempt by others to obtain a court order for removing the life supports failed. Three days later the woman dies. The futility of maintaining life supports was a strong probability, but neither the medical team, the husband, nor the courts could predict when death would come.

The second condition where probability of recovery is practically nil is when there are repeated cardiopulmonary resuscitation (CPR) efforts. How often should the CPR team resuscitate the patient before the procedure becomes an exercise in futility? What are the ethical issues involved in a physician issuing a "Do Not Resuscitate" order? At what point in such cases does futility set in?

A third highly improbable situation is the extent to which physicians can use extrabody membrane oxygenation to maintain heart and lung function while the patient awaits a heart transplant. Doctors say that this method can be used to maintain heart and lung function for "up to several weeks." Calculating the probability of how long life can be sustained affects decisions about the use of the technology.

In all three of these cases, the matter of probability is at stake. These physicians say, "Futility is almost always a matter of probability." However, they say that the probabilities that such attempts to sustain life will be futile cannot be determined statistically.[3]

However, the probability of recovery or death at the point of first appearance of the disease can be calculated in terms of the chances, or odds, of recovery or death. One medical condition in which probability of cure is statistically predictable is cancer. People tend to consider all cancer as terminal, but this is not the case. According to the *Mayo Clinic Health Letter,* a wide range of probabilities of cure have been in existence since 1970. Since then, the probabilities of cure have increased in different kinds and locations of cancer (see table 1).

By "cure" is meant that the person has survived for five years without reoccurrence of the cancer after the initial treatment. The *Mayo Clinic Health Letter* says further: "More than seven million treated for cancer are living today. More than five million have passed the five years milestone. But doctors monitor well beyond five years after treatment." The odds of recovery are well above 50/50. However, the odds in cancer of the brain are 22 out of 88, or 1 out of 4; in cancer of the stomach, 18 out of 82; in cancer of the esophagus, 5 out of 95; in cancer of the pancreas, 3 out of 97.[4]

Probability of Physician "Mistake"

Such optimistic or pessimistic odds make for a fragile relationship between physicians and their patients. The probability of mistakes by doctors in making decisions based on such calculations, to my knowl-

Table 1
Probabilities of Cure in Specific
Kinds and Locations of Cancer

	1970s	1980s
Testicle	63%	92%
Melanoma	60%	81%
Bladder	53%	79%
Breast	63%	78%
Cervix	58%	67%
Prostate	50%	75%
Colon	43%	57%
Hodgkin's lymphoma	40%	76%

edge, has not been studied statistically. Physicians expect perfection of themselves and permit themselves no mistakes. For example, Dr. David Hilfiker reports giving routine prenatal care to a young mother. All the laboratory tests indicated that the fetus was dead. He gained the parents' permission to remove the fetus and did so, only to find that it was alive. He was overwhelmed with grief. He checked with the pathologist again and was told that the four negative pregnancy tests he had analyzed could not possibly have been wrong. He told the parents what had happened. They were good friends of his as well as patients. He had no excuse for not having done an ultrasound, which would have verified the life status of the fetus. Yet they were understanding and noncondemnatory of him for the mistake.

He, however, could not forgive himself. He felt guilty and angry. He recounts other mistakes and near misses he had experienced in his practice. He notes that he did not feel it possible to discuss his mistakes with another physician. He says that mistakes by a physician are treated as if they are sins. Yet there is no one to whom he can confess, seek comfort, and find companionship as he works through the guilt and anger he feels.

He relates all of this to the present surge of malpractice cases. The couple did not choose to sue him, even though the aftermath of the disruption of the pregnancy caused considerable suffering for the mother. She was unable to conceive again for two years.[5]

My own guess is that the couple did not initiate a malpractice suit because of the personal relationship they had with the physician. He did not seem to be hurried or impersonal in his care of them. In contrast, one report says that the average length of visits of physicians with patients is seven minutes! Other reports draw a direct connection between impersonal and even anonymous relationships between physicians and the incidence of malpractice suits. Even so, the physician can rightly say that he or she is primarily responsible for accuracy and perfection in the use of the technology of medicine and in paying attention to his or her care of the patient. Some assume having a "good bedside manner" is of secondary or even tertiary importance. Careful attention to technique does lessen the probability of mistakes. Hence he or she does not leave to luck the accurate use of all known procedures while taking time to make friends with the patient.

In such a climate of demanding perfection, the physician makes no room at all for probability, bad luck, or mistakes. Nevertheless, in dealing with diseases physicians are in a world of probability. Their patients are repeatedly asking them what their chances are, what the odds are that a given surgical procedure, for example, will succeed.

A doctor is not a superperson, but is like other people—imperfect. However, when going into surgery, an act of faith steadies both the doctor and the patient. The important thing is the attitude of patients in regard to the outcome. If they perceive themselves as losers who are always the victims of bad luck, their outlook is poor. If their outlook is optimistic and they know other patients were winners in their "betting their lives" on a given surgeon, their chances are better.

Such a form of gambling goes on with more or less intensity in hospital rooms or treatment rooms on a regular basis as the probabilities of success are measured again and again. The probability of death in the case of an AIDS patient is ultimately 100 percent. Table 1 above, which gives the probabilities of recovery of different kinds of cancer patients, indicates, in gambling lingo, the odds in the success rate of cure of cancer. The Christian believer in providence makes note of the probabilities, but puts his or her faith, not in probabilities, but in his or her inseparability from the love of God in Christ Jesus our Lord (Rom. 8:39). Hope is not confined to this life only.

Probability and Life Habits

Closely related to the rates of cure and surgical success are the life history and habits of the patient. Consider, for example, a patient in the hospital who is seventy-four years old. He has survived a heart attack. His parents lived to be in their nineties. Their personal habits history was excellent except for a high-fat diet. However, he is a heavy drinker, and he smokes heavily, two packs a day. His family genetics have enabled him to live into his middle seventies. Nevertheless, the probability of death coming earlier to him than to his parents is high because of his habits.

Our habits along with our genetic family history have a strong influence on the probability of health or disease and, ultimately, on the number of years that we live. For example, the incidence of lung cancer among women has increased 300 percent since 1970. For a woman to refrain from smoking decreases the probability that she will develop cancer. Liver and heart disease are either exacerbated or directly caused by the abuse of alcohol. Knee and ankle disease, heart disease, and diabetes are either caused or complicated by overeating and resulting obesity. Yet these unhealthy habits are rampant in the whole population. Abusers point to George Burns, who smokes many cigars a day and is above ninety years of age. They trust that they will be as lucky as he is. They trust in luck to make them an exception to the health statistics while they indulge in unhealthy habits. They need all the luck they can get. Such people attempt to substitute luck for personal discipline, calculation of risks, and the elimination of unnecessary chance and disaster.

Another example of the importance of habits is seen in young dropouts from school. The formation of good habits of study, prompt preparation of assignments, and consultation with teachers about their progress are not a part of their set of habits. In the absence of instruction in the home, their peer group provides such guidance as they get. In very few peer groups is it "cool" or the thing to do to be a good student. To do so is to be able to tolerate some ridicule, to stand alone, and to chart one's own path. For many this is too much, and unhealthy habits take over—hanging out with the gang, staying out late at night and not doing homework, and having a very active social life.

Driving habits are another crucial part of a person's habit history. The person who forms healthy habits of driving becomes a safe driver. Speed limits and stop signs are there to shape healthy driving habits. Seat belts and air bags are there to reduce the possibility of fatalities in case of an accident. The habits of wearing seat belts and using air bags have reduced fatalities from 54,633 in 1970 to 46,900 in 1989, according to the National Safety Council. Mirrors are there to let one know what is behind one. Directional signals and brake lights are there to communicate intentions to other drivers. The persons who form healthy habits use these devices and do not trust to luck to keep them safe.

Conversely, persons who form unhealthy habits of driving ignore speed limits, stop signs, and other traffic instructions. They do not wear seat belts, nor do they insist that passengers in the car do likewise. These persons trust to luck to take care of them in spite of such unhealthy driving habits. The probabilities of death or being severely disabled in auto accidents are increased by aggressive driving habits or by driving while under the influence of intoxicating beverages. The chances taken by a drunken driver account for twenty-one thousand deaths by accident. The probabilities of accident are decreased by defensive driving and/or by complete sobriety while driving. In either instance, safety in driving is increased by knowing the probabilities. There was a drop of nine thousand fatalities between 1970 and 1975 when the speed limit was nationally lowered to fifty-five miles per hour. With the return to sixty-five miles per hour, we are seeing an increase in automobile accident fatalities. Luck and probabilities are not only a matter of individual faith; they are important in establishing national policy.

The development of healthy habits amounts to ruling out the elements of unnecessary risk, chance, and misfortune, calculating carefully the nature of necessary risks and making provisions for them, and asking whether the chances of failure justify the effort.

The person who has healthy habits has little need for luck. The person who has unhealthy habits makes of luck a secular faith. To put it another way, we have a great penchant for making our own good luck or bad luck depending upon the quality of our habit formation. The person with faith in God in Christ combines the careful calculation of necessary risk and probabilities with prayer to God in Christ, who manifested courage in the face of certain death.

Probability and Sampling

In July 1992, when the presidential campaign was in full swing, one report of a sampling of voters' preferences stated the following:

A new poll published yesterday by the Washington Post and ABC showed [Bill] Clinton with a slight lead of 33 percent to 31 percent for [Ross] Perot. [George] Bush was preferred by 28 percent. The poll, conducted June 24–28 among 785 registered voters, had a margin of sampling error of plus or minus four percentage points, meaning that it recorded a practical dead heat.[6]

The poll was inconclusive, but it does show that the country was badly divided as to whom people wanted for president *at that time.* It would take four more months of grueling campaigning and the voting on the first Tuesday in November to reach a definitive conclusion. The calculation of probabilities before the election is always uncertain, for later events show how quickly polls can be outdated. Polls have a very transient life.

However, the science of polling has become precise enough that an agreement had to be reached with the media that they would not predict winners and losers until the western states, three hours later in time than the east coast, would have the opportunity to vote.

In the earlier days of predicting probable victories, an embarrassing reversal took place in the election of Harry Truman. People went to bed as the morning papers were being printed announcing Thomas Dewey the winner of the election only to awaken to the reality that Truman had indeed won. More recently, a less dramatic but equally upsetting election occurred in the Israeli election of Yitzhak Rabin of the Labor Party over Yitzhak Shamir of the Likud Party. Here again the limitation of polls to predict the outcome was evident when they showed a close, toss-up race that in reality turned out to be a landslide victory for the Labor Party.[7]

Even though every effort is made to take the guesswork out of political activity, much of it is still a matter of high probability and sheer luck. To participate in politics even at the minor office level is to subject oneself to chance and to gamble at best. It takes a lot of secular faith in luck to engage in it.

Parapsychology and Probability

Research into parapsychology is another arena of human life where probability theory has been used. Parapsychology includes at least two areas of experience: extrasensory perception and psychokinesis. Extrasensory perception refers to a human being's ability to obtain information without using his or her senses or logical deductions. It occurs outside the accustomed ways of knowing. Psychokinesis is the apparent or real ability of a human being to move objects or people around him or her without touching them physically but by the force of his or her thought processes only.

Both these phenomena require the persons' belief in themselves and their capacities. None of this belief is attributed to God or to any manifestations of God's power. They are based on the credo that a given individual is endowed with special powers that other people do not have.

These phenomena and people's belief in them have a long history that preceded scientific experimentation such as we have today. As early as 550 B.C. in Greece, the oracles Amphiaraos and Delphi were tested by King Croesus of Lydia. He wanted to know whether he should go to Persia and attack Cyrus. He followed the Oracle of Delphi's word: "When Croesus has the Halys crossed, a mighty empire will be lost." The oracle did not say *which* empire would be lost. Croesus lost. This story reported by Herodotus is considered the very first parapsychological experiment on record.[8]

Since that time, nonexperimental expressions of parapsychological phenomena have recurred throughout history. For example, there have been the studies in animal magnetism by Franz Anton Mesmer in the 1760s, Emanuel Swedenborg's spiritualism and his belief in conversations with the dead, and the persistent work of mediums who have purported to have precognitive abilities to predict events and to arrange séances with the dead. In 1882 the Society for Psychical Research, headed by a respected Cambridge University professor, emerged with the purpose of scientifically exploring the validity of psychical phenomena and the claims of those experiencing them. The methods of research were imprecise, using anecdotes at worst and case history at best.

Finally, the precise, rigidly scientific, and experimental era of parapsychological studies was ushered in by more than one research center in this country. The Duke University Parapsychological Laboratory had its origins in 1929 when J. B. and Louisa Rhine were invited to Duke by William MacDougall, the head of the psychology department. He offered J. B. a professorship in psychology in 1928–29. That led to the founding of the Institute for Parapsychology at Duke University. Also, at Princeton University the Princeton Engineering Anomalies Research Laboratory is investigating parapsychological phenomena. At the Stanford Research Institute, a physicist has conducted research in this field. In Great Britain, the Parapsychology Laboratory at the University of Edinburgh is an endowed program of research.

The work of J. B. Rhine is illustrative of the nature of the research. He had five different symbols printed on twenty-five different cards. They were obscured from the subject of the research project. The objective of the experiment was for the person to determine what the symbols on the cards were without having seen the cards.

The element of chance identification, the probability, had to be assessed. The question was, Can this subject identify the card more often than chance would allow? The standard chance factor is one in twenty. If a person accurately identified the cards with a score of seventy-five, then he or she would be functioning well beyond the chance factor. This person would be exceptionally clairvoyant in comparison with a less successful person. In other words, he or she could anticipate probabilities with a foreknowledge that other people cannot. With remarkable precision, it seems that, ruling out chance factors, some people are luckier than others in their capacity to outwit probabilities. None of these persons claimed divine guidance in their responses.[9]

We can appreciate the precise work of the parapsychologists in university laboratories. They have demonstrated quantitatively that some persons are more intuitively independent of their senses than others in the acquisition of data. They are more skilled at anticipating probabilities than others. Clairvoyance, the ability to perceive future probabilities with precision, has been demonstrated on case-by-case research. However, the leap of surmise of mediums, fortune-tellers, and soothsayers of all sorts is still a secular faith in assessing the good or bad luck of its adherents. Psychical research in the communication with the dead continues as more of a faith commitment without reference to God, a secular faith.

AN ADVENTURE IN PROBABILITY

A humorous set of probabilities surrounds the human responses to the absence of heat or light and the end of war. In colonial America, a couple would keep warm by "bundling." They got into bed together fully clothed to keep warm and at the same time to have privacy from the rest of the family. They could talk privately, cuddle, and kiss. Parents often would put a bundling board between them to assure a measure of safety from pregnancy. Nevertheless, the probability of pregnancy was evident in the number of "six-month children" born six months after the wedding. The probabilities of conception in bundling could be measured by these "six-month children." As one family physician commented, "All children of married folk take nine months except the first one."

A similar demonstration of the probabilities of conception occurred after the great blackout of electricity in New York City several years ago. Nine months later there was an outstanding increase in the number of births. The absence of light left more time for sexual relations between husbands and wives, intimate couples cohabiting, and casual acquaintances in the same dark space. The probabilities here were similar to those in bundling.

Another such evidence of the probability of the birth of babies was reported after the return of the military men and women from Desert Storm. Nine months later there was an increase in the number of births.

One would have to have individual knowledge of each couple in all these responses to the absence of heat or light and the end of war to know whether these couples thought the births were good or bad luck or a gift from God. In all three instances, the probability of the conception of a child with an increased number of times of sexual intercourse—in cold of winter in New England, in the dark of New York's blackout, or in the celebration of homecoming—was predictable with few intervening variables.

CONCLUSION

Throughout this chapter we have seen the scientific commitment of research persons to control the variables between a present situation and the probabilities of a desirable outcome. If they can identify and control the variables, they can improve the lot of humankind, granted that the scientific efforts are being done by people who have humanitarian goals for their work.

However, it has been seen that knowing the variables and controlling them is a very relative and not absolute endeavor. Some scientists become messianic and assume that they can ultimately control all variables to the degree that they have substituted grandiosity for serious empirical research. They assume the possibility of their omniscience. Even if this were possible, they would be bound to a certain place of geography. They might be able to control the variables and invent the medicines to cure leprosy. However, they could not get that medicine to the millions of children in Third World countries. They would have to be omnipresent as well.

Even if they could do this, they would remove the risk of one dreadful disease from the world, but they would have only touched the hem of the garment of the massive numbers of risks that all of us take every day. They would have relieved us of the courage that it takes to live in a risky world. They would relieve us of the necessity to discipline ourselves with wisdom in the choice of healthy habits. They would have taken from us the necessity of faith. That faith would be a faith in luck if we are secular-minded persons, or it would be a faith in the wisdom of God as we consider the probabilities of life with its hazards and hopes.

6. Gambling

*T*he secular faith in luck is not simply floating around in the thin air of a secular culture. It has heavily committed devotees who attend and practice its rituals in specific powerfully funded temples and storefront churches dedicated to people's faith in luck. Some of these places of worship observe the separation of temple and state. Others are operated by the states themselves. I need only name Las Vegas, Atlantic City, Monaco, and other such places to give the reader a vivid picture of what I mean by those temples that practice the separation of temple and state. Furthermore, simply to mention state lotteries makes it clear what I mean by storefronts, because lottery tickets are sold in stores. However, neither kind of place of devotion could exist unless persons themselves were not already devotees of gambling as a way of life. They espouse a faith in the assumption that money is central and can be gotten in a few moments in time, and without working. Therefore, in this chapter we will deal first with the history and nature of gambling, then with the dynamics of the devotion to gambling, and finally with the temples and storefronts of organized gambling.

A HISTORICAL PERSPECTIVE

The English verb "to gamble" has a recent origin. It dates back to the Revolutionary War, 1775–83, although it has roots in Middle English and Old English. However, the commonly understood meaning of gambling refers to the betting or staking of something of value with the express intention of running a certain risk in hope of gaining more value in the outcome. The results, or outcome, of gambling are governed by the ratio of chance or odds. These may or may not be known by the gambler. They may be deliberately and mathematically set by the operators, or "priests," of the gambling temple.

The act of gambling is not of recent but ancient origins. Evidences of gambling have been found in ancient Britain, Greece, Rome, Egypt, and American Mayan cultures. Six-sided dice have been around since long before the birth of Christ. The earliest ones are from Iraq and India. Casting of lots was used as a means of ending disputes, dividing or distributing property, or determining what was God's will. All four Gospels mention the casting of lots to decide on the distribution of Christ's clothing after his crucifixion.

Ethnographers have studied the presence or absence of gambling in different cultures. Among the nongambling societies are aboriginal Australians, Polynesians, Micronesians, some Indonesians, most Siberians, and many East Africans. They also include the cultures of much of South America, except Peru, highland Bolivia, Chile, Argentina, and Paraguay. One study of fifty tribes from all over the world showed that forty-three played games of physical skill, twenty played games of chance, and nineteen played games of strategy (such as chess).[1]

The long history of gambling leads one to assume that the propensity to gamble has deep and even primitive roots in both the personal and racial subconscious of the human race. Its fascination for some people is a mystery wrapped in an enigma, although as we will see, some psychoanalytic studies have taken modest steps in unwrapping the mystery wrapped in the enigma.

DEVOTEES OF GAMBLING

Although gambling can be seen as a deeply entrenched belief system—a secular faith in luck—the large majority of gamblers are not fanatical followers of the faith. Some gamble once or twice a year while on vacation or a trip to Las Vegas or Atlantic City, the way some church members attend church services on Easter and Christmas. Others gamble professionally and make their living at gambling, just as churches and denominations have large contingents of "full-time Christian workers." Others are compulsive gamblers, just as some persons are addicted to a particular form of religion.[2] Religion can become compulsive, legalistic, and uncontrollable even as gambling can be. Not all gamblers are the same, even though many Christians are "teetotalers" when it comes to gambling. Most do not look kindly upon any form of it.

Fun-Loving Gamblers

Many people indulge in gambling only on special occasions, primarily for the fun of sharing in a pastime with friends and associates. For example, Christians and unbelieving secularists gather in backyards on Derby Day in Louisville to watch the Kentucky Derby run on television. A backyard betting pool is formed, and people who never bet at any other time do so for fun. When Derby Day is over, they never think about gambling again until the next Derby Day. If they win, they congratulate themselves on being lucky, for they know little or nothing about horses and the secrets of "the odds." Very strict religionists would call this a terrible sin that separates one from God. However, common sense would see it as a fun-filled pastime.

Large sections of the Christian community use the game of bingo as a fund-raiser for churches and other charities. The player in a church-sponsored game is more likely to feel he or she is a "righteous gambler" who gets a little fun out of being "taken" by the church. However, even bingo has a darker side. State regulations put no limits on the number of bingo cards a person can buy. The gaming institution can "pay out as little as a third or less of the take. As a result one should only play bingo for charity and expect to lose money—with little risk of disappointment."[3] Just as the state wrings money from willing hands that will not willingly pay taxes, charity organizations wring money from the hands of people unwilling to give to them out of the largess of their hearts and the conviction of the worthiness of the cause. Also, more people are likely to become addicted to bingo than to other forms of gambling.

We have already mentioned "vacation gamblers." During a vacation of a week or ten days, these people allot a certain amount of money for gambling. They determine ahead of time how much they will let themselves lose. They spend money this way as recreation and take winning or losing philosophically. If they win, they have a free vacation. If they lose, they at least enjoyed the vacation away from the cares at home.

Professional Gamblers

The second major type of gambler is the professional gambler. The professional gambler has studied, researched, and calculated the odds in a game of chance. He or she then plays the game according to this knowledge. The result, however, is that the professional gambler can make a living at "taking" the recreational "suckers" who have not taken the time to be as skillful as he or she is.

The professional gambler usually turns to games in which skill, reasoning, and inside information play a part along with luck. They do not depend on luck entirely, although they invest a lot of faith in luck. Because of their close study of the game, the professionals are also thoroughly versed in the ways of cheating on the system. The casino gamblers have at least seventy-eight ways to cheat, even sometimes at the risk of their lives. More often they are thrown out of the establishment.

GAMBLING AS AN ADDICTION

Unfortunately, some people cannot be considered either amateur fun-loving gamblers or professionals. They become compulsive addicts driven by an irrational set of unconscious forces. The structure and meaning of gambling addiction can be understood best by first studying a classical case history of an addicted gambler. One of the most well-known gamblers is Fyodor Dostoyevsky (1821–81), the Russian novelist, author of such works as *The Brothers Karamazov, The Idiot,* and *Memoirs from the House of the Dead.* He always had trouble with money even when he had money to spare. He had many years of severe financial distresses. When his beloved brother Michael died in 1864, he took the responsibility for supporting Michael's wife and children. Fyodor could hardly support himself. In a dire circumstance to stave off a creditor who had threatened to foreclose on him, Dostoyevsky employed the star pupil of Russia's first shorthand school and in four weeks dictated to her for transcription the 160 pages of a short story entitled "The Gambler." (She continued to work for him, and later he fell in love with and married her. She was his steadfast comrade in his writing career.) He earned enough money from the story to pay off his debts.

The central character of "The Gambler" is Alexis Ivanovich. He is a mirror image of Dostoyevsky as a gambler. Jessie Coulson, the translator of "The Gambler," says in the introduction: "Alexis, the narrator of the novel, is undoubtedly a self-portrait, or rather a reflection of two sides of Fyodor Mikhailovich's temperament and personal history, one that of the gambler, the other embodied in the hero's relations with and feelings for Polina [his beloved]."[4] Probing this character's thoughts and motivations reveals some of the dynamics that drive devotees of gambling.

Alexis is a tutor with a gathering of well-to-do people who are on vacation in Roulettenburg, a gambling resort. Dostoyevsky has his spokesman tell of two different kinds of gamblers: (1) The rich and privileged who gamble as an amusement and quit when they have had their fun. They are the "gentlemanly gamblers." (2) The vulgar and mercenary gamblers who gamble as disreputable persons. One gets the impression that he saw himself as a vulgar person who gambled to grasp the most money in the least time with the least effort. In his words: "Russians also need money, and so we are very glad to have, and very addicted to, ways like for example roulette, of getting rich quickly, in a couple of hours, without working. It's a great temptation to us; and as we play without purpose or effort, we lose everything we possess."[5]

Alexis Ivanovich decided that he could not play roulette for someone else. He said he was "absolutely sure that when I begin to play for myself (and I have twelve friedrich's d'or) I shall win. . . . I am utterly sure . . . that as soon as I begin to play for myself I can't fail to win. . . . I only know that I *have* to win."[6]

Later, in watching an elderly woman of their company who was quite wealthy win repeatedly, Alexis became overwhelmed. For him the die was cast: "I was a gambler myself; I realized it at that moment. My arms and legs were trembling and my head throbbed."[7]

The story ends with his saying: "Tomorrow, then, —oh, if it were only possible to leave tomorrow! To be restored to life, to rise again. . . . I have only to stand firm but once, and I can change the whole course of my destiny in an hour!"[8] Such is the life of the gambler. Today we would say that Alexis Ivanovich was addicted. We have intensive therapies for this addiction. We have Gamblers Anonymous, just as we have Alcoholics Anonymous. Dostoyevsky describes in detail the grip that gambling can hold upon a person. He looked upon it as a kind of death of the real person. His hope lay in a resurrection. But for the gambler with one gulden in his pocket, that will be tomorrow. Shakespeare, in *Macbeth,* put it this way: "Tomorrow, and tomorrow, and tomorrow, creeps in this petty pace from day to day, to the last syllable of recorded time, and all our yesterdays have lighted fools the way to dusty death" (Act 5, Scene 3).

CLINICAL ASSESSMENTS
OF COMPULSIVE GAMBLING

Dostoyevsky rejected the thought that he was committed to understanding the depths and agonies of the human spirit. Yet his dramatic portrayal of the gambler captures the imagination and increases the empathy of the person related to a compulsive gambler in a way that clinical psychological and psychiatric assessments do not. One does not need the training and certifications of psychology and psychiatry to understand and use his wisdom.

However, the criteria and the more systematic treatment approaches of the psychologist and psychiatrist are more precise. Their understanding and empathy for a compulsive gambler are less impressionistic and intuitive. Therefore, a composite of this wisdom is valuable in understanding these full-time devotees of luck, these worshipers of the secular faith, luck.

In *The Psychology of Gambling*, Edmund Bergler makes the same distinction between gamblers as did Dostoyevsky. Some people gamble as a fleeting pastime and do not incorporate it into their way of life. The "once-a-year" gamblers on the Kentucky Derby and vacation gamblers are examples of this type.

Bergler then discusses the pathological gambler. This person makes gambling a way of life. He or she is chronically and repetitively involved in gambling. Gambling "absorbs all his [or her] other interests like a sponge." He or she is "pathologically optimistic about winning and never learns his [or her] lesson when they lose." Compulsive gamblers eventually risk more than they can afford. Also, they "enjoy an enigmatic thrill which cannot be logically explained, since it is compounded of as much pain as pleasure. Punishment and pleasure are blended in the same act at an irrational, unconscious level."[9] Dostoyevsky describes this enigmatic thrill thus:

> Feeling as though I was delirious with fever, I moved the whole pile of money to the red—and suddenly came to my senses! Fear laid its icy hands upon me and my arms and legs began to shake. With horror I saw and for an instant fully realized what it would mean to me to lose now! My whole life depended on that stake![10]

He won that time.

Bergler says that three conscious justifications form the basis of the compulsive gambler's outlook on himself or herself and the world: (1) They are "subjectively certain that [they] will win"; they "just know." (2) They have an unbounded faith in their own cleverness. (3) They "claim that life itself is nothing but a gamble." This composite is the stuff of which the devotee of luck as a secular faith is made.[11]

Whereas the conscious intention of the pathological gambler is to win, he or she is driven by unconscious forces to lose. The following sets forth Bergler's primary hypothesis:

> All aggression is paid for by some form of self-punishment. . . . [T]he gambler cannot win in the long run. For him [or her] losing is essential to . . . psychic equilibrium. It is the price he [or she] pays for neurotic aggression, and at the same time it makes it possible . . . to continue gambling.[12]

He adds another dynamic in the gambler's unconscious. He or she is unconsciously and aggressively getting back at his or her parents for their work ethic. Although the gambler's parents instilled in their child the axiom that only honest work brings success, gambling seems to prove the opposite—one can get rich with no work at all. Thus gambling becomes a means of refuting the parental injunction that logic and justice rule in the world. To gamble is therefore a way to turn against the parent: "You claimed that in the best of all worlds nothing is left to blind chance. . . . Blind chance does rule in many places and I intend to take advantage of it."[13]

In today's world the clinician sees gamblers, who as are other kinds of addicts, parasitically dependent upon the addiction. This perpetuates a dependent way of life and short-circuits an interdependent maturity on their part.

The *Diagnostic and Statistical Manual of Mental Disorders* of the American Psychiatric Association suggests the following diagnostic criteria of pathological gambling, four of which must be present to make such a diagnosis:

1. Frequent preoccupation with gambling or with obtaining money to gamble
2. Frequent gambling of large amounts of money over a longer period of time than intended
3. A need to increase the size or frequency of bets to achieve the desired excitement
4. Restlessness or irritability if unable to gamble
5. Repeated loss of money by gambling and returning another day to win back losses ("chasing")
6. Repeated efforts to stop gambling
7. Frequent gambling when expected to meet social or occupational obligations
8. Sacrifice of some important social, occupational or recreational activity in order to gamble
9. Continuation of gambling despite inability to pay mounting debts, or despite other significant social, occupational, or legal problems that the person knows to be exacerbated by gambling.[14]

Four psychiatric treatment modalities for the pathological gambler have been identified:

First is psychodynamically based psychotherapy. The results have been uneven. Bergler lists five cases that were definitively recovered. He says that out of sixty gamblers whom he has treated in analysis, about 8 percent have recovered.[15] Even so, psychodynamic therapy seems to be our most fertile source of understanding these persons.

Second is Gamblers Anonymous, modeled on the pattern of Alcoholics Anonymous, which depends upon inspired membership in a group of fellow sufferers. Results are good if the person stays in the group, but the dropout rate is very high. The important thing to note about this organization is that it is free, and desperate gamblers are usually without funds. Probably the gamblers with affluent relatives are the ones who get psychodynamic treatment.

Third, clinical psychologists have experimented with behavior modification approaches that have had success as equally modest as the other approaches.

Fourth is the recognition that an addiction follows a predictable pattern that in itself is mysterious. For example, to what extent is addiction genetic, the result of life's stresses, or at first a voluntary and then an organic effect? All of the above is a good answer. Gerald G. May, M.D., tells of three cases of addiction—one to compulsive sexual behavior, one to alcohol, and one to the stress of a business career. All three genuinely wanted to be free of their addictions. They moved beyond willpower and their disciplines of reformation and were met by a mysterious grace that delivered them. They said that they "just quit." They did not shift to another addiction. From a medical point of view, these would be seen as spontaneous recoveries. Yet a careful inquiry into the other forces going on in their lives at the time might reveal how life itself became the therapist.[16]

THE TEMPLES OF LUCK
AND STOREFRONTS OF LUCK

Bergler says that gambling games fall into three categories. First are games of pure chance, such as roulette, dice, screeno. However, our study of probability makes it very clear that *pure* chance is a fiction. The statistical odds in these games are well known to the "priests" who run the gambling temple (or casinos). The second category includes games in which chance is combined with skill, reasoning, "inside information," and the ability to bluff. Bergler names the stock market, poker, and horse racing as examples. Third, there are games of pure reasoning, such as chess.[17]

Whatever the kind of game it is, great temples of gambling attract devotees of gambling. Gambling has its institutions and places where devotees express their faith in luck in the rituals of elaborate casinos, racetracks, and storefronts where lottery tickets are sold.

Casinos

Las Vegas is America's gambling mecca, but it was not always so. In 1855 the Mormons built a fort at that spot to aid in their missionary work with the Paiute Indians, the Native Americans who were living there. The site was later bought by the railroads in their push westward. The city was founded in 1905 and chartered in 1911. In 1931 gambling was legalized. After the Hoover Dam was built in 1936, the resulting growth and the influx spurred by the gambling industry combined to produce what is now a city of 258,295 in the most recent census.

Las Vegas has the reputation of being "the city the mob built." "Bugsy" Siegel, a noted underworld character, built the first hotel and casino, a glittering place called the Flamingo. He appropriated funds furnished by the mob and was assassinated for doing so on June 20, 1947. Although state officials set up rules for keeping the mob out, they have not been successful in doing so.

The Internal Revenue Service requires the casinos to give an accurate account of all winnings. They do so in a scrupulous manner. However, they pay off winners in cash. As one executive is quoted as saying: "You win a million dollars, we give it all to you. We get ironclad identification and even take a color photograph of you, but then we hand over the money—no checks, all cash." Why cash? "If we give you cash, we stand a good chance of getting at least some of it back immediately."[18]

The city is largely composed of two areas of hotel-casino temples— the downtown and the "Strip" area. Carl Sifakis insists that the Horseshoe, located downtown, is "all that a gambler could want. . . . [T]he Horseshoe will cover any bet of any size [and] . . . lets the player set his own limits. Whatever he bets on his first wager . . . becomes his limit."[19] The "temple" itself sets and controls the ratio of odds in such a way that it is assured a profit, and at the same time the players win often enough for them to continue playing.

Las Vegas is the largest but not the only gambling center in Nevada. Reno is a little city by comparison with Las Vegas. Lake Tahoe adds to the attractions of gambling the natural beauty, skiing, and water sports of the area.

Atlantic City, New Jersey, competes with Nevada for first place in gambling. However, it has been called "Dullsville by the Seashore" in comparison to Las Vegas. The constant criticism of this temple of luck is that when the casinos were first built, there were promises that gambling would make Atlantic City prosperous. Instead, it has become a high crime area, and 90 percent of the city's businesses have vanished. Nevertheless, "Atlantic City's 11 hotel-casinos in 1985 reported earnings of $2.2 billion—a half-billion more than the total earnings of Las Vegas' 60-odd licensed establishments. . . . The secret is that Atlantic City has had 30 million visitors."[20] Atlantic City easily draws patrons from Boston, New York, Philadelphia, Baltimore, and Washington. Altogether, it has a one hundred million population base from which to draw.

The drawing power of these temples is awesome. They do not have to undertake "outreach ministries" to recruit followers. The primitive urges of faith in luck within people's inner psyche push them to the glittering promise of these vanity fairs. The promise is that money is to be had in a very brief time without working. People go with the same fever that Dostoyevsky had—the fever of not only the conviction that they can win but also a lurking unconscious need to lose.

Racetracks

Racetracks can also be considered as temples populated by devotees of gambling. In my own city of Louisville, Kentucky, is one of the world-famous racetracks, Churchill Downs. Although the first week in May is the famed Kentucky Derby week, this week is both preceded and followed by several weeks of racing. Another season of racing is held in the fall.

Here the devotee of racing adds to the element of chance an array of knowledge that enables him or her to estimate with varying degrees of accuracy which horse is most likely to win. Some factors are these: (1) The genetic line of the horse's sire and dam is an important factor. The offspring of outstanding winners like Secretariat or Seattle Slew are considered to be more likely to win. (2) The winning horses in previous races have a record that increases the chances that they will win in an upcoming race. (3) If the trainer of a horse has a long record of successful winners, he or she will likely produce more winners. (4) The jockey's record of winners, years of experience, stability, and other such factors are factored into the calculations of a possible winner. (5) Inside information about the health and stamina of the horse on the day of the race always helps to sharpen the edge of the devotee's calculations. Much of this information is found in daily publications such as daily racing forms and guides, stud books recording heredity lines, and related information. Other variants are considered such as track condition, the length of the particular race as matched with a particular horse, and post position in the starting gate. Worthy of note is that Churchill Downs earned $43,700,000 in 1991.

Storefronts

Thus far we have been talking of "temples" for devotees of gambling. However, state lotteries are not held in centralized "temples."

Lottery tickets are sold in grocery stores, drug stores, liquor stores, service stations, and a variety of other storefront locations. The devotees of luck in Kentucky who played the lottery spent $425,000,000 in 1991! At present in the United States we have thirty-nine state lotteries.

Modern state lotteries in the United States began in 1963 in New Hampshire. I will restrict this brief discussion of lotteries to the United States, although more than fifty countries have lotteries, including Great Britain, Germany, Italy, France, Ireland, Turkey, Spain, China, Poland, Thailand, and some countries in South America. Lotteries are not new in the United States. "From 1776 until 1820 over 70 lotteries were authorized by Congress for public works."[21] In 1990 there were seventeen states with lotteries, although in these days of tight state government finances and voter refusal to accept taxation, more and more states are starting lotteries to supplement state budgets. However, in my own state of Kentucky, which started a lottery in 1988, a considerable amount of mystery surrounds the exact uses made of lottery money. No public accounting of these funds is forthcoming.

The payoffs in lotteries can be exceptionally large, mounting into the millions. Or they may consist of the small return from "rub-off" tickets in which instant payment is made if the numbers under the covering material match in a variety of ways. Thus players either win big or win small. Even an occasional small win induces players to continue to play. One of the major criticisms of lotteries is that they bleed those least able to spend money gambling. They are the poor person's mode of gambling. However, whereas other forms of gambling are readily subject to cheating by the skilled gambler, the lottery is not easily open to cheating. States all know that much of the money spent on lotteries is from welfare checks. As Carl Sifakis says, "In many states the very check cashing establishments that cash welfare checks also sell lottery tickets, a sort of on-site banking for the poor."[22]

Another dimension of the inequity of the lottery system is that even though persons may win millions of dollars, that money is not paid out in one lump sum. It is paid out in annual installments over a period of twenty years. Then it is taxed upon receipt. The person cannot, therefore, invest the money in a lump sum and earn interest from it. To the contrary, the state invests it and earns the interest. Sifakis points out: "There is much to be said for the idea that if a Wall Street promoter represented a stock deal the way the states do their lotteries he would most likely be put behind bars."[23]

CONCLUSION

In 1988 the overall expenditure on gambling was $151,440,000,000. In 1993 the expenditures were over $330,000,000,000. The power of luck as a secular faith energizes this massive expenditure. Several final observations can be made as to the existential situation of the way of life of the devotees of gambling.

First, gambling is a *lonely* way of life. The temples and storefronts are highly organized and form an incredibly large company of conferees in community with each other. Their patrons, however, pursue a lonely existence. If they win, they have hangers-on who surround them as long as they have money. If they lose, they lose alone.

Second, the impelling force that prompts the gambler is a *fantasy* that they are an exception. Only others lose; they win. In terms of existential psychotherapy, we could say that they perceive themselves as being special. Not even losing punctures this fantasy with reality. The hidden contempt for work and for those who work for money is another expression of this sense of being special. They feel they are different from, other than, and superior to the common mortals who submit themselves to the drudgery of work. Delayed gratification is foreign to them, and their sense of being special convinces them that instant gratification in winning is their destiny in life. When they win, they win *now*!

Finally, *greed* fuels the temples, the storefronts, and the bingo halls. Greed is essentially a commitment to the shortcuts in life. The epitome of this commitment is the Greek myth of Midas, who asked that everything he touched would turn to gold. He got his wish. Even his food and drink turned to gold, so he starved! The lonely, fantasy-ridden, and greedy existence of the gambler leads to a kind of death. The gambler stakes his or her life on the way of life of faith in luck.

Part 2

Responses to Luck
by Pastors and Churches

7. Pastoral Responses to Secular Faith in Luck

*T*he preceding chapters of this book have discussed the secularization of belief in the providence and deliverance of God into a faith in luck. Although this issue is important, it is not one to which a busy pastor usually gives high priority. Pastors have hospital calls to make, committee meetings to attend, sermons to prepare, consultations with individuals and families about crises in their lives, funerals to conduct, and the care of their own families to consider. They have little time to stand back from all these duties and reflect upon the implications of the idea of luck as a secular faith.

Therefore, the purpose of this chapter is to relate the propensity of people in the church and even pastors to live fatalistically, to take chances, to try to figure out probabilities, and to gamble in any of a myriad of ways. Pastors are called to respond to this secular faith in luck in their teaching, preaching, exercise of pastoral care, and administrative leadership as well as in their personal lives.

THE PASTOR AS A THEOLOGIAN AND TEACHER

As we study the scriptures, we see that Jesus was seen as "Teacher," or "Rabbi," more often than not. He told parables based on the common experiences of his hearers, such as children playing in the marketplace, the beating of a person on the Jericho road who was cared for by a Samaritan tradesman, the sight of lilies in the field, or the building of a house. He helped his followers relate such everyday experiences to the traditions of their scripture, our Old Testament, and the will and purpose of God.

One of the reasons such theological considerations as providence, deliverance, and hope have been secularized today is that the interpretation of them has been allowed to go by default to advertising agencies, pop psychology help books, and television gurus. The majority of these sources of instruction fail to deal with the profound questions people raise about their relationship to God. Furthermore, the identity of pastors as teachers gets lost in the uproar of many conflicting voices.

Although preaching has an important role, the pastor who attempts to do serious teaching from the pulpit in sermons faces an uphill effort. The sermon form itself is a one-way form of communication. People cannot raise questions. The setting and time constraints of the sermon form do not permit this. Recently I heard of a pastor whose sermon was interrupted by a man standing in the audience and remonstrating her. His actions created a severe alarm in the congregation. The man's sanity was questioned.

However, if we change the context from a regular morning worship service in a middle-class church to a congregation of mental patients in a hospital, a dramatic change occurs. The chaplain preaching there *expects* to be interrupted. While serving as a chaplain in a mental hospital, I preached at a Mother's Day service. I chose my text from Mark 10:7, where we are told to leave father and mother to be joined in marriage, and compared it to Matthew 19:29 in which we are told to leave father and mother to become followers of the Lord Jesus Christ.

In the middle of my sermon a woman in the audience stood and asked, "Preacher, all that sounds well and good, but what if it is not in a mother to do it?" I stopped my prepared message and spent the rest of the time responding to her. I began by saying: "That is the most important question to ask. Many mothers don't 'have it in them,' or, to put it another way, do not have the spiritual strength to let their children grow up, take up their crosses, and follow the Lord Jesus Christ. They want children to meet their needs, to do and to be with them." Instead of allowing me to just glorify motherhood, this woman had pushed the discussion to the deeper level of considering the lack of emotional and spiritual strength many mothers feel.

Yet this turn of events could not have happened if she had not been permitted to raise a question during the sermon when it was most pressing. This incident suggests the value of pastors' creating teaching and learning situations in which genuine dialogue can occur. I commend the model of Frederick W. Robertson, a nineteenth-century English pastor. He preached a worshipful and persuasive sermon in the mornings and gave a lecture in the late afternoons each Sunday. In these lectures he raised serious theological questions about the issues of the day. He probed and enriched the belief systems of his people. He responded to their questions and clarified his own thinking and that of his congregation at the same time. He found, as I have, that more people attend a dialogue session than they do a sermon.

When pastors actualize their function as theologians and teachers regarding the secular faith of luck, they need to be prepared to face such questions as these:

1. Does God have complete control over the world and our lives?
2. Is God limited to the creation that is still in process?
3. Does God cause everything in our lives? Is the world also filled with chaos as well as divine order?
4. Is faith in luck a secular way of making peace with chaos, poor odds, and pure accidents?
5. To what extent do we make our own bad luck?

A pastor does not need to have immediate answers to all these questions. He or she can note them and promise to study them and discuss them at another time. Certainly, as a theologian and teacher in the parish, a pastor can probe the substance and meaning of secularization, which means life lived on a horizontal plane without reference to the vertical dimension of faith in God. This book could be used as a study guide for a series of sessions on these issues.

THE PASTOR AS A PREACHER

The placement of the discussion of teaching before preaching may reflect my predilection for teaching rooted in my lifelong work as a teacher both in theological and medical classrooms. Even so, let me express my lifelong affection for being a preacher as well as a teacher. I have preached and published numerous sermons. However, I have not, except for six years in the pastorate, had the responsibility for preparing two to three sermons a week. I am aware of the enormity of such a task and have great admiration for those who accept this huge challenge.

In the New Testament, although Jesus was recognized as a rabbi, or teacher, the apostle Paul was the first and preeminent proclaimer or preacher of the gospel. The church throughout the centuries has placed great importance on the preaching role. Today many more people are likely to hear sermons than to participate in discussion groups in churches. Therefore, it is important to address luck as a secular faith through the proclamation of the gospel in pastoral sermons.

The whole idea of luck is both a new and an old one to the average congregation. The dangers of a secular faith have often been identified in sermons. Secularism is like a creeping rust in the girders supporting the proclamation of the gospel. Yet the idea of luck as a competitive faith is not often addressed in contemporary preaching. How then shall a pastor deal with such an unfamiliar issue?

A sermon with lighthearted recounting of several instances of faith in luck from the daily newspaper will provide an attention-getter from the start. Usually, these stories reflect a curious blend of a religious faith with a firm amount of belief in luck. For example, consider the experience of Pat Day, the jockey whose horse, Lil E. Tee, won the 1992 Kentucky Derby (see chap. 2). More recently, I heard on the morning news about three teenage girls who broke the boredom of an afternoon by walking on a railroad trestle in rural Kentucky. A train entered the bridge, trapping them. They survived by clinging with hands, arms, and feet to the railroad ties and the outside guardrails. One of them said of the harrowing escape: "*God* saved us this time, but we would not be so lucky a second time!"

Another example is the event of an earthquake centered near Killari and Umarga, India, in which approximately sixteen thousand persons were killed on September 30, 1993. The previous day the region is reported to have observed a day of respect for the god of luck.[1]

The sermon can then note: "One reason luck is barely noticed as a secular faith is that it is so pulverized with superficial awareness of God that we think nothing of it."

The scriptures can be searched for examples of luck and fortune-telling. Saul's experience in 1 Samuel 1:28 is a case in point (see chap. 2). Jesus prepared carefully to enter Jerusalem (Luke 19:28–36). He also used this careful foresight and planning in preparation for the Passover meal that would be his last supper (Luke 22:7–13). He did not leave these critical events to chance or luck (see chap. 1).

Sermons following the introductory one could take up the following topics:

Belief in Fate or Belief in God: The sermon can contrast faith in God in Jesus Christ as our provider with dependence on luck (see Genesis 22 and 1 Cor. 10:13).

God and Christ as Our Strong Deliverer: God in Jesus Christ can deliver us from despair in the clutch of fate (Ps. 103:1–8; Deut. 5:15, 6:4–9; Gal. 1:3–4—"who gave himself for our sins to set us free [deliver] from the present evil age, according to the will of our God"). The confusion of the sacred with the secular creates much, but not all, of the problem with luck as a secular faith.

Taking Chances in a Pushy World: The experience recounted in Daniel 3:13–18 can be used as a way of separating the belief in luck from an unqualified belief or faith in God. Even more challenging to faith are the questions Jesus asked in the garden and on the cross.

Calculating Probability in Times of Crisis: Another approach is the recognition that humankind's struggles with estimating probabilities of death in the face of disease are very present to many people today. The issue can be discussed in a delicate, yet profound way because the possibility of life or death is real to many. The consideration of the probabilities of death from cancer is an example of this concern (see chap. 5).

Why Does a Good God Permit Suffering? or *Are Accidents Always Planned by God?* These are questions that can be pondered in sermons as well as in the group discussions suggested above.

The Nature of Gambling and the Present-Day Epidemic of Gambling: Many social ethics issues revolve around the epidemic of legalized gambling sweeping this country today. Americans gambled about $80 billion dollars in 1986 and $330 billion dollars in 1993. By 1993, thirty-nine states had lotteries, nine allow casinos, and sixteen have federally approved casinos on Indian reservations. Gambling in casinos and lotteries is touted as a substitute for taxation. The proceeds will ostensibly go for supporting education. The lottery in Kentucky was sold to voters with that promise. Yet the universities have had several across-the-board cuts since those promises were made.

Why the Church Should Oppose Gambling: Discuss several ethical issues at stake in gambling, such as the following:

1. *The deception* involved calls up memories of Jesus' discussion of the "father of lies," as is evident in John 8:39–47. This passage raises the question of a doctrine of Satan. Here Satan, the devil, is personalized as a liar, the father of lies. We miss the point when we etherealize Satan and overlook his or her incarnation in people who lie.[2]
2. *The desire for money without working* is an important part of the appeal of gambling (see chap. 1).
3. *The parasitism of gambling,* especially on the working poor, needs to be addressed. They will buy lottery tickets when their "chances" of winning are 1 in 64,000,000. Casino gambling produces no food, clothing, gasoline, and but few jobs.
4. *The threat of addiction* is inherent in gambling, just as it is in the use of alcohol and other addictive drugs.[3]

THE PASTOR AND CARE OF PERSONS

The pastoral care of persons in the congregation is a third important responsibility of pastors, along with teaching and preaching. Pastoral care is offered on many levels. The daily interaction between a pastor and the people of the congregation prepares the ground for the more intensive exercise of pastoral care during times of sickness and bereavement or when people seek counseling.

Daily Pastoral Relationships

In casual or relatively unstructured conversations, pastors can communicate attitudes and challenge conventional wisdom about the role of luck in everyday life. Such encounters can also model ways laypeople can minister to one another as they struggle with the decisions that are part of daily experience.When we consider such issues as weighing the odds, taking chances, considering probabilities, we are often involved in what the Bible calls temptation—or testing—as the crucible in which our character is formed.[4] When we lift the innermost parts of our decision making to God in Jesus Christ by asking for the guidance of the Holy Spirit, we have the assurance offered by Paul in Romans 8:26–27:

> Likewise the Spirit helps us in our weakness; for we do not know how to pray as we ought, but that very Spirit intercedes with sighs too deep for words. And God, who searches the heart, knows what is the mind of the Spirit, because the Spirit intercedes for the saints according to the will of God.

We decide in the inner depths of our being whether to trust God to provide for us or to play the odds, the chances, and the probabilities, and thus to gamble. In both instances, the odds, the chances, and the probabilities are there. In the presence of God, they are temporal, creaturely realities. In a secular faith, they are imagined to be infinite, yet in our control. However, in such a context we are alone in facing them.

Not only is a secular faith in luck a lonely venture; it is also filled with illusions that provoke anxiety over the outcome of the gamble. The act of faith that places the outcome in the care of God in the Lord Jesus Christ generates serenity and enables us to function at the maximum of our capacities. As a side effect, this empowerment improves the outcome and enables us to survive. The grandiosity of the gambler is forfeited for serenity of faith in God. This pours forth from the act of surrender of the outcome to God. As is expressed in the prayer often attributed to Reinhold Niebuhr:

> God, grant me the serenity to accept the things I cannot change, the courage to change the things I can, and the wisdom to know the difference.

Awaiting such an act of surrender of our self-sufficiency and grandiosity is the unmerited grace of God as our Lord Jesus Christ. As Gerald May says: "Addiction cannot be defeated by the human will acting upon its own, nor by the human will opting out and turning everything to the Divine Will. Instead, the power of grace flows most fully when human will chooses to act in harmony with God's Will."[5]

May's phrase "when human will chooses to act in harmony with God's Will" means to me that we consider the chances, the odds, and the probabilities of life in any given situation. Then we "wait for the Lord," as in Isaiah 40:31, and new strength, wisdom, and direction will come to us at the center of our being. This shifts decision making from the secular to the sacred, from loneliness to companionship, and from anxiety to serenity. Thus we are at ease with God and readied to interact with other family members or church members.

The Care of the Sick and Bereaved

The care of the sick and bereaved involves two issues often blended with the secular faith in luck. First is the matter of dealing with the probabilities that a patient will live or die: "What are his or her 'chances' of living or dying?" Second is the issue of theodicy: "Why did God let this happen to me? What have I done to deserve this?" If the patient does not ask such questions, the family probably will.

These two kinds of questions may be directed openly to the pastor. A more difficult situation arises when the individual or the family bluntly claims that God has betrayed them. For example, when I was a very inexperienced pastor, six months after I had officiated at the marriage of a young couple, the bride had an attack of appendicitis. At that time no antibiotics existed. She developed an infection after the surgery and died quite suddenly. Her funeral was a time of heartbreaking, wrenching grief for her family.

I went to the home after the funeral to comfort the family. The father was filled with rage. He said: "She was sick. You prayed for her. She died. You can take your damn God and go to hell with him!" I was flabbergasted and speechless while the mother and sisters tried to intervene. I do not recall *any* defense or response I had to make to the man! I have never felt as inadequate since!

As I look back on this crucial human situation from the angle of vision of luck, a secular faith, I am impressed by how the passing of fifty years has changed the probabilities in such a case. Today this patient would have been given an infection-killing antibiotic prior to her surgery. Peritonitis, the infection of the peritoneum, the membrane lining the abdominal and pelvic walls, would have been readily prevented and/or cured. The patient's probabilities of recovery would be 95–99 percent, whereas in 1942 they were much less. Was this danger the luck of the times? Or was it the lack of knowledge of human disease? Or did God *do* this to her and especially to her angry, brokenhearted father?

Today I would have told her father that he had every right to be angry at me, at God, and everyone else he wanted to be. However, I would have told him that God is more ready to accept his anger than anyone else because the ignorance and evil of the human race had killed *God's* own son. Then I would have asked him to permit me to share his rage about the death of his daughter. I would have stayed with him and shared in his rage and grief; I would not have left him. Yet that is what I did at the time. I still wonder if he finally rationalized this tragedy as a very bad streak of luck, ill-fortune, fate, when the odds were against him.

Formal Pastoral Counseling

Formal pastoral counseling as done by a pastor of a church is usually crisis intervention counseling. The pastor can often meet these challenges with the help of others who are specialists in a wide range of therapeutic, legal, occupational, and business areas. If these people are not members of the church, they are in the larger community. After the initial stages of the crisis are over, a pastor can refer the long-term counseling needs to these persons.

Yet the pastor tends to be, after calls to 911, the first person who is called, especially in such matters as marital and family problems. Persons in such situations may think their luck has run out or has turned against them. Their confidence in their own skills in controlling the probabilities in their lives has come to an end. To be sure, few people seek any kind of counseling until they have tried everything else! Their secular faith in luck has let them down. They are like the sailors in Shakespeare's *Tempest* amid a tempestuous noise of lightning and thunder. These mariners, in their desperation, cried: "All lost! to prayers, to prayers! all lost!" (*The Tempest,* Act 1, Scene 1).

In such a frame of mind, counselees tend to expect another form of luck from pastors—magic! Yet pastors are not magicians. They are persons of prayer when they are at their best with desperate people. The presence of the pastor provides another person to share the load. When a joy is shared by another, it is multiplied by two; when a sadness is shared, it is divided by two. Pastors do not perform magic, but they provide community for that other person. Similarly, they represent the presence of the living Christ. In doing so, they offset the severe isolation that people who put their faith in luck tend to experience.

Sometime in the counseling session—after a sense of trust has been established—the issue of depending on luck can be contrasted with forming a steadfast fellowship with the God and Father of our Lord Jesus Christ. The cleverness, the isolation, the loneliness of the luck-driven can be put aside for a companionship with the Suffering Servant. It may well be that the sufferer is groping for this kind of relationship more than for sudden magic or a set of tidy answers. Then the particulars of her or his suffering can be confronted in the hope of God's provision and deliverance. Then, as Robert Browning put it in his "Prospice," written upon the occasion of the death of his wife: "For sudden the worst turns the best to the brave."[6]

In such a walk of life with a counselee, the despair of fate is displaced by a courageous outlook on the future. The self-sufficient cleverness of the secular believer in luck is set aside for a confidence in the God of our Lord Jesus Christ.

THE PASTOR AS A LEADER

Another task of the pastor of a congregation is that of being a leader. The act of being a leader is often erroneously called "administration." Both in the sacred and secular world, the word *administration* has collected some well-deserved disdain. The former president of Union Seminary in New York, John Bennett, once told me: "I am not concerned with administration, but I am deeply concerned about the leadership ability of our graduates!"

As a leader, the pastor seeks to identify the special skills of the lay leadership in the church. He or she searches for persons who can form a team to do the works of love in the name of the Lord Jesus Christ and of the church. A favorite aphorism is "Every member a minister in his or her own way and every pastor a coach." To recognize persons with leadership ability requires one to take time to get acquainted with the membership of the church in more than a casual way.

The situation becomes more complex if the church has several staff members in addition to the pastor. Forming a team of cooperative spirits with high morale is a challenging task. Clarifying each staff member's job description is very important. Otherwise, staff members who have no sense of the boundaries of their work may begin to exercise leadership inappropriately in the life of the church.

The roles and functions of committees become important, especially as they relate to the official boards. There is much wisdom in the comment of John Schwab, chairman of the Department of Psychiatry at the University of Louisville. He said that he preferred to have as few committees as possible because they easily develop a separate life of their own. He preferred task forces to do a specific job and then to be dissolved when that job was completed.

Wise leadership is a strong counter to a secular faith in luck. Although such matters may seem to be mundane issues within the sacred life of the congregation, they form *the very arena in which one may begin to gamble.* The pastor may, by default, leave the leadership of the church to chance and coincidence. Leadership may receive attention only when an interpersonal crisis gets in the way of teaching, preaching, and pastoral care. As time goes by, many power vacuums are apt to form. By the very nature of the case, if no one is designated as leader, someone else gets drawn into the empty places. Very soon, the fellowship of the church gets into gamesmanship and gameswomanship, as Eric Berne describes it. The games "Uproar," creating confusion over irrelevant issues, and "Let's you and him/her fight," the deliberate setting of people against one another, appear.[7] All too rapidly these mundane issues take over, and many people in the church follow the pastor in taking chances and gambling away the energy, the vitality, the financial stability, and the attendance of the congregation.

The pastor, therefore, has an important function as a leader and coach of the team of the church in creatively working with others to fulfill the mission of the church, as well as to offer leadership in the larger community.

THE PASTOR AS A PERSON

Finally, trusting in luck as a secular faith can secularize the very person of the pastor in the life of the church. The pastor himself or herself faces dangers if important matters of personal care are left to chance.

Stress Management

The work of a pastor, the way he or she functions in the church, involves his or her being "on call" twenty-four hours a day, seven days a week, three hundred and sixty-five days a year. In contrast, in the medical professions, where health emergencies abound, a system of sharing "on call" is almost universal. Thus stress that cannot be ended permanently can be interrupted regularly. Yet pastors customarily accept the expectations of perpetual motion that churches tend to have for them. Once when I was a professor of psychology of religion and pastoral care at a seminary, I received a telephone call at about five o'clock in the afternoon at home. Our sons were quite young, and I was playing with them while my wife was preparing dinner. The caller was a distraught woman who was phoning from the airport immediately after deplaning. She said that she was in a lot of trouble, needed to talk with me, and asked if she could do so that evening. I told her that I had been working since seven-thirty that morning and that evening was the only time I could be with my family on that day. I hastened to say that I could see her the next morning at nine o'clock. Would that be acceptable? She readily said, "Certainly," and added that she would be visiting friends that evening.

She came promptly the next morning. The first thing she said was: "I have been a pastor's wife for several years. I have never heard him or any other pastor place their fellowship with their family ahead of responding to an emergency call until you did so last evening. This is one of the reasons I am upset."

This was a stressful situation, but the one called to be a pastor to this woman had to distinguish what was a real emergency from a perceived one. No life-and-death situation existed in her case. It was a chronic distress, not an emergency.

Creating space and time for the intimate nurturing of one's spouse and children also returns nurture to the former. Not to do so is taking chance after chance, gambling away the opportunity for renewal in the everydayness of ministry.

Isolation

Another way that pastors take chances with their own well-being is by letting themselves become increasingly isolated from a spiritual support system within the church and community. A poignant example of this was Elijah when he fled the city after his triumph over the priests of Baal. He met God at Mount Horeb. In his depression he told the Lord: "Take away my life." Then he lay down and slept. The messenger from God awakened him later and saw to it that he was fed. Elijah then poured out his complaint to the Lord. In turn, God sent him to Elisha, who would be his understudy and disciple. God assured Elijah of his safety and pointed him to a company of "seven thousand in Israel, all the knees that have not bowed to Baal, and every mouth that has not kissed him" (1 Kings 19:4–18). His isolation, loneliness, and despair were met as he interrupted the stress of his isolation by presenting his plight to God.

In addition to turning to prayer, a pastor will do well to pick three or four of the wisest and most dependable persons in the church to help her or him monitor the workload on a regular basis, at least once a month. This group could be asked to serve for a stated length of time; then others could replace them. Furthermore, staying in weekly touch with the chairperson of the vestry, session, council, or deacons enables a pastor to know what issues are emerging before they become news after the fact. This preparedness takes some of the element of chance out of the life of a pastor. Jesus advised his disciples to become "wise as serpents and innocent as doves" (Matt. 10:16b). Pastors can stop gambling with their own health and well-being by building a support system of people within and outside the church.

Finding others who share in the ambiguous situations a pastor faces is another important source for a life support system. Staying in touch by long-distance telephone can bridge the miles if the others live far away.

Pastors may find such support among friends in the congregation as well. The adage that a pastor cannot have close friends in the parish situation is a half-truth, the worst form of a lie. A pastor and his or her spouse can have many close friends in the congregation. However, there is great danger when one person or one couple absorbs *all* the time available for friendship with the pastor and spouse. These liaisons can become a reckless form of taking chances for high stakes. They may easily slide down a slippery slope into a sexual affair. A pastor may insist that such a relationship is his or her own private business. Nevertheless, a pastor is bound by covenant with the larger community of the church. New covenants with a paramour cannot safely be formed at the expense of the prior covenant with the church. To do so is to gamble with one's own life as well as the life of one's family and that of the paramour in a very chance-driven way.

Pastors as well as others run the risk of becoming conformed to this world, of being secularized, when they gamble with their luck. In Romans, Paul warns about being conformed to this world. He calls all Christians to "be transformed by the renewing of your minds, so that you may discern what is the will of God—what is good and acceptable and perfect" (12:2).

8. Congregational Responses to Secular Faith in Luck

*I*n the last chapter, the role of the pastor in responding to luck as a secular faith in his or her teaching, preaching, pastoral care, and giving leadership in the church was considered. The pastor's need to be intentional about his or her own personal life was also discussed. This chapter takes up ways that the congregation can be involved in responding to luck as a secular faith. In particular, suggestions will be made about (1) helping families respond, (2) wisely handling the resources of the church, and (3) addressing community concerns about organized gambling.

LUCK AS A SECULAR FAITH CHALLENGES THE FAMILY

Consider the story of the rich fool. When Jesus was asked to mediate a dispute about division of a family inheritance, he told the story of a man whose fields provided an abundant harvest. All the barns were full, and more had to be built to hold the harvest. The man was feeling very smug and secure with all that he had. Jesus then posed the question: "The things you have prepared, whose will they be?" In the context of the parable, the answer is: "They will be things over which your heirs will fight!" (see Luke 12:13–21).

Many people fantasize about having a rich relative die and leave them a large inheritance. That will be their big break. Thus they will get money without working. This desire to receive without expending effort is the beating heart of gambling and the secular faith in luck— getting money in a moment's time without working for it.

If the family can be the seed plot of gambling, it can also be the first line of defense of the Christian fellowship against the secular faith in luck.

I remember visiting for a week in the home of a maternal uncle who was a farmer. He had five teenage children. After the simple evening meal of buttermilk and cornbread, my uncle and aunt gathered us all in a sitting room for spiritual conversation. This experience was new to me. I grew up in a single-parent home where my mother, sister, and grandmother tried to civilize the three of us who were brothers. My mother, sister, and grandmother were godly people, but such conversation about spiritual things happened only on an unplanned basis.

The present-day home is far more like the home I grew up in than like my uncle's home. Several realities in the nation make this so. In many families, both parents have to work to maintain the family's standard of living. In many homes, there is only one parent; thus there is no possibility of conversation among adults in the home unless grandparents or at least a grandparent lives in the home. Indeed, "More than one-fourth of all American babies are now born to single mothers."[1]

These circumstances provide a background for appreciating profoundly conversation of any kind, especially spiritual conversation in the home. When a family converses spiritually in the home, a remarkable event is taking place in spite of the adverse social pressures, the omnipresence of television, and preoccupation with blaring contemporary music from the radio.

Any discussion of luck as a secular faith in the home is extremely unlikely. Yet many Sunday school and church programs assume the pattern of the nuclear family such as my uncle's family of sixty years ago. As a teacher of mine used to say, "There is only one thing wrong with that; it is not so." How then can families be encouraged and helped to talk about the hazards of luck as a secular faith?

A series of sermons on "Faith in Luck or Faith in God" could prepare the way (they might draw upon the topics suggested in chap. 7). In a second phase, the pastor could meet with the heads of households and encourage them to study and discuss the subject at home, using as resources the following material about God as provider versus faith in luck as experienced in the Christian family. Families can talk about their experiences in relation to luck, God's provision, and God's deliverance.

Getting any study going in the home between parents and children may be difficult. Nevertheless, if even five or ten families take this process seriously, at least they will be aware of and give thanks for God's role in their lives. A pastor can be grateful for the families who take the time to study these issues at home. The whole matter of fate, taking chances, defying the probabilities, and gambling can even provoke laughter in the process of learning. If this approach of home discussion does not "fit" in some congregations, the materials can be used in study groups in regular programs at the church. I am hopeful that family conversation can be started. In spite of the upstream effort against the current of social forces, spiritual conversation *can* occur in the home.

God as Provider and Deliverer

The main emphasis in such conversations should be placed on God as provider and deliverer in the daily needs of life and the recurrent crises in family life. Much is said about the providence of God in theological literature. The following scriptures can become topics for home conversations.

Genesis 22:1–14 is the dramatic story of God's providing a sacrifice in place of Abraham's son, Isaac. Abraham named the mountain where this happened *Jehovah Jireh,* or "on the mount of the Lord it shall be provided." This passage could stimulate much discussion if discussed in an "unpious" way. For example, where was Isaac's mother, Abraham's wife, while all these events were happening?

Job 38:41:
Who provides for the raven its prey,
    when its young ones cry to God,
    and wander about for lack of food?

Psalm 65:9 is a prayer to God:
You visit the earth and water it,
    you greatly enrich it;
the river of God is full of water;
    you provide the people with grain,
    for so you have prepared it.

Psalm 78:20 raises a doubting question about God's continuing care:
"Even though he struck the rock so that water gushed out
    and torrents overflowed,
can he also give bread,
    or provide meat for his people?"

Luke 8:3: This passage tells the story of how Mary Magdalene and several others whom Jesus had helped provided for Jesus and his disciples out of their resources. One of the main ways God provides for us is through other Christians who have been helped.

When we turn to the letters of Paul, we find a fresh, new emphasis on God as our provider, relieving us of the necessity of a secular faith in luck.

1 Corinthians 10:13: "No testing has overtaken you that is not common to everyone. God is faithful, and he will not let you be tested beyond your strength, but with the testing he will also provide the way out so that you may be able to endure it."

The word "testing" can be also translated "temptation." A good conversation starter for a family is to go around the circle and ask what temptation—that they can talk about—bothers them most. You might also compare this passage with Abraham's testing in Genesis 22. Also, what are the main temptations each family member struggles against to keep from gambling on his or her luck?

2 Corinthians 9:8: "And God is able to provide you with every blessing in abundance, so that by always having enough of everything, you may share abundantly in every good work." God not only provides for our needs; God enables us to share with others.

1 Timothy 5:8: "And whoever does not provide for relatives, and especially for family members, has denied the faith and is worse than an unbeliever."

These are some of the scriptures that reveal God as our *Provider.* The Bible also portrays our God as *Deliverer.* We have some narrow escapes in life. At these times we are apt to consider ourselves lucky and thus confirm our secular faith in luck. The thought of our escape as deliverance by God is not usually considered. However, such experiences of deliverance are a core concern in the Old Testament, especially in the Psalms, but also in Proverbs and the Prophets. A concordance will list many references to the word *deliver.* A brief selection follows:

Psalm 33:18:
> Truly the eye of the LORD is on those who fear him,
>> on those who hope in his steadfast love,
> to deliver their soul from death,
>> and to keep them alive in famine.

(This passage can be related to the story of Joseph and his brothers in Egypt in Genesis 37, 39–50; especially 50:20).

Psalm 34:4:
> I sought the LORD, and he answered me,
>> and delivered me from all my fears.

(This verse can be related to 2 Timothy 1:7: "For God did not give us a spirit of cowardice, but rather a spirit of power and of love and of self-discipline.")

Psalm 39:8:
> Deliver me from all my transgressions.
> Do not make me the scorn of the fool.

(Relate this verse to the Lord's Prayer in Matthew 6:7–14.)

Psalm 56:13:
> For you have delivered my soul from death,
>   and my feet from falling,
> so that I may walk before God
>   in the light of life.

(Compare this verse to the story of Jesus' healing of the Gerasene demoniac in Luke 8:26–39.)

These are just a few of many psalms that can be related to the New Testament and to narrow escapes experienced in modern life. Families can recount narrow escapes they have known. Did these events teach them to "fail-safe" their lives from then on? Or did these experiences increase their recklessness? Did they thank God and take heart for God's deliverance?

These passages of scripture provide a pattern for discussion of the difference between a sacred and a secular faith. All people inevitably face fateful experiences. They daily deal with chance, cope with the odds, and calculate the probabilities of life and death. When they treat these situations in light of a secular faith—gambling with chance, the odds, and calculating the probabilities apart from the providential care of a faithful God—they have a lonely, self-centered, fate-driven life. Yet to experience life as persons who commune with God and neighbor in prayer about these issues opens up a world of meaning.

Faith in God's deliverance from death keeps our feet from stumbling and enables us to walk in the light of the Lord, not as victims of the hazards of luck.

The Christian Family Converses

In these days of the privatization of religious experience, people often become quiet when faith in God is mentioned. Yet, when the local lottery or the referendum on casino gambling is up for discussion, everybody has an opinion. With the help of material in this book, conversations can be pushed to a deeper level concerning faith in luck. In a family setting, a father or mother can raise some of the following issues for conversation over a period of time.

The family is a bundle of habits. Chance taking in the face of known probabilities is a form of gambling. Indulging in habits such as smoking, drinking alcohol, and making junk food a large part of the diet are examples of such gambling. The discussion of life habits in chapter 5 will provide material for family discussions on this subject.

Money and work are indissolubly connected. Gambling at the races, the casinos, and the lottery all hold out the promise that large sums of money can be obtained in a moment of time without working! This is a secular faith.

Over against this illusion is the biblical understanding of the provision of God for our basic needs: food, clothing, shelter, and protection from severe heat or cold. All these take money—money earned legitimately by working. As the family sits down to a meal together, an event that happens on purpose and is not left to chance, these basic provisions are all present. They did not happen by chance. Purposeful and steady work produced them. The lesson can be reinforced by giving thanks for the work that paid for and prepared the food on the table.

Foremost in a teenager's thoughts is how he or she can get money. The first option is often to ask the parent to provide funds for all the youth's wants, not needs. This is the teachable moment. A parent can ask in return how the teenager can fulfill these *wants* while the parent provides the necessities of life. As I write, the temperature outside our home is twenty-two degrees below zero. Snow is sixteen inches deep. Yet a young teenager delivered our morning paper to our front door! He has learned the connection between work and money. One can thank God for providing work for him to do and for his commitment in doing it.

This paper delivery person is a stark contrast to those who patronize the casino gambling centers that are now selling their establishments to whole families. They have, in connection with their casinos, elaborate entertainment centers rivaling the Disney centers. The children can play while the parents gamble. "What does gambling have to do with children? Note the number of children's arcades and fast food restaurants that are building the gambling habit into playtime and mealtime activities."[2] Gambling is a way to get money in a moment of time without working. What an illusion to be taught to children and youth! (See chapter 1 for further discussion of this issue.)

Driving the car is another encounter with fate or chance. When we take the wheel, we may not consciously calculate the odds or the probabilities of a car wreck that may take our lives. We increase the risk by not wearing seat belts and taking too casually the privilege of driving. When the teenager gets a set of car keys, a time of prayer is appropriate. The prayer should include thanksgiving that God has provided work to earn money to pay the costs of the car, the training that prepared the driver to use the car, and the driver's intelligence and wisdom to use the car, deathly instrument that it is, wisely and carefully. The prayer can then focus on God's deliverance, asking God to deliver the driver from any temptations to drink alcohol or use drugs, especially while driving this car. Such a prayer takes chance, the odds, and the probabilities out of the hands of a secular faith in luck and puts the matter in the hands of God as Provider and Deliverer. (See chapter 5 for further discussion of this issue.)

Sexual activity is another arena in which faith in luck often reigns supreme. People too frequently take chances with unplanned pregnancies and the probability of contracting a sexually transmitted disease. Usually the first disease that comes to mind is AIDS, communicated through both heterosexual and homosexual sex as well as shared illicit drug use. Rarely now do persons even think of other sexually transmitted diseases, some of which chronically reappear, such as chancre sores, chlamydial infections of the urethra, gonorrhea, nonspecific urethritis, syphilis, vaginitis, genital herpes, and hepatitis B.[3]

All of these diseases await the person who has sex with strangers and outside committed monogamous relationships. In no other area than promiscuous sex is faith in luck more obvious or fraught with the naive assumption that an individual is an exception to the laws of probability. (See chapter 4 for further discussion of these illusions of safety.)

THE LOCAL CHURCH AND
LUCK AS A SECULAR FAITH

The church, in addition to the home, can work with the pastor to set aside the secular faith in luck and begin to discern ways of the church that need mending and transforming under a providing God who delivers us from destruction.

How Churches Gamble

Churches have a way of gambling with their financial resources—not at a casino, a lottery, or any such thing—but in the undiscerning chances the leadership takes with the budget. For example, in a time of economic recession, the church's leaders may call for approval of a budget 10 percent greater than last year's budget even though the last year's budget went into deficit.

Or the leadership might propose an extensive building program that may be based on the assumption that the congregation will double its membership in the next ten years. Yet the surrounding community consists of lower-middle-class people who will likely move into a distant community when their incomes increase. Building a sanctuary, let us say, to seat 1,650 persons when the church has only 1,000 people present at Easter and Christmas, with a regular attendance vacillating between 500 and 700, is risky indeed.

These are ways that unthinkingly the leadership of the church literally gambles away the financial stability and membership future of the church. The leaders incur large debts for building; however, young couples on limited incomes are smart enough to know that they cannot afford to belong to a church that much in debt!

The Problem of Organized Gambling

Apart from the fiscal behavior of the church, the ethical and political issues of gambling in the community around the church call for concerted thought and action.

The first question to ask is whether the church itself uses gambling devices such as bingo and raffle prizes with which to pay the expenses of the church. These are widespread practices for financing the church. The practice of luck as a secular faith is at full tide in the hope that winners will get something quickly for very little money and no work. At the very least, these practices should be reexamined, especially in light of 2 Corinthians 9:5, where Paul speaks of giving what has been "promised . . . as a voluntary gift and not as an extortion."

On matters of financial support, the pastor is often bypassed in decision making, or decisions like these are sometimes made when the church is without a pastor. The burden of responsibility, in any instance, rests upon the shoulders of lay leadership.

The church needs to focus on the waste and wreckage of human life that is a consequence of gambling. Gambling is a pastime that can turn into a profound addiction or pathological gambling. "In 1986, 3 million

Americans were compulsive gamblers. Today (1994) Gamblers Anonymous estimates 6 to 10 million."[4] The *Diagnostic and Statistical Manual of Mental Disorders* describes pathological gambling: "The essential features . . . are a chronic and progressive failure to resist impulses to gamble, and gambling behavior that compromises, disrupts, or damages personal, family, or vocational pursuits. . . . Problems that arise as a result of gambling lead to an intensification of the gambling behavior."[5] (See the more detailed listing of the criteria of pathological gambling in chapter 6.) The waste of money, indebtedness, inability to repay debts, and stealing checks or writing cold checks all are a part of an addiction to gambling. (See pp. 71–75. Also, more information on this can be obtained by calling Harbour Center in Baltimore, Maryland, at 410–332–1111 or Gamblers Anonymous at 213–386–8789, or by writing Gamblers Anonymous International Service Office, Box 17173, Los Angeles, CA 90017.)

A crucial time comes in the life of both the church and the community as a whole when legalized gambling through casinos, lotteries, and bingo halls becomes a political issue. In such circumstances, both the pastor and the membership of the church have a political stake in what happens. In addition to the issues previously named—deception, the desire for money without working, the parasitism of gambling, and the threat of addicting part of the population to gambling—there is also the infusion of leadership from outside the community. Gambling institutions are often operated by strangers to the community. The possibility of these outsiders bringing organized crime with them is very high. Other accompanying malevolent forces, such as prostitution, the influx of drugs, and the involvement of minors in these trades, add to the urgency of voter opposition.

The task of political action calls for a church to join forces with other churches and all organizations that are opposed to legalized gambling. Here liberal and conservative, mainline and fundamentalist, sophisticated and unsophisticated, all have a cause in common.

An editorial in the *Christian Science Monitor,* often called the most objective newspaper we have, titled "Gambling's False Promise," calls attention to the siren call of casino gambling and tribal bingo on Indian reservations in this country. Add to these the increasing numbers of "legalized state lotteries, parimutuel betting, sports betting, and gambling in Las Vegas and Atlantic City, and the question is: Who isn't gambling these days in the United States?" On Indian reservations gambling is called the "new buffalo."

Just as the four-legged creature provided ample substance for Indian tribes of old, profit from gambling does the same today. . . . We share the opinion of a few tribes that what the buffalo helped give, the casino takes away: identity, purpose, grace and heritage. . . . [T]he property gambling is offering is built as such. The market for casinos is close to being saturated. Casinos are likely to fail because of this. . . . There are rumblings that organized crime may be involved on a few reservations.[6]

Gambling is the rawest example of luck as a secular faith. The institutions of gambling are a drain of $330 billion on the American economy. That money would go a long way toward reducing the national debt! Therefore, the action of the church as political force is imperative. The pastors and lay leaders of churches can function effectively in at least two ways. First, they can speak in community gatherings as well as preach from the pulpit to inspire opposition. Second, they can privately confer with influential persons in and out of public office to enlist their assistance in opposition.

Even so, a pastor and church should not become focused on any single issue. Gambling is but one issue. There are many others calling for the prayerful concern of Christians who trust in God to provide for them and deliver them from evil.

Epilogue

*F*ew people have recognized luck as a faith, and a secular faith at that. Yet, when a calamity such as a nine-year-old son's being hit and killed by a car going fifty-five miles an hour in a twenty-five-mile-an-hour school zone occurs, the grieving parents ask, "Why did God let my son be killed?" It will be some time before they can accept the fact that accidents do happen. Their concerns about luck *and* providence collide. One prays that they will come to know that God will provide them energy, hope, and courage to go on living in spite of their grief.

Yet the force of secularization has pushed such concerns as these out of the consciousness of most people. They turn to the legal system to pursue the driver of the car as a criminal for murdering their son. Their anger is vented toward him, not God, and for certain, they do not look for God's providence to help them through their grief. They cope with their grief in a good luck/bad luck way. Chance and accidents are accepted stoically, and they rely upon their own strength to pull them through. They have a secular faith in good luck and bad luck, which means that God is not operative in their grief situations.

A gradual process of secularization has pushed aside the distinctly religious interpretation, function, and ritualization of life. Life is seen as controlled by an impersonal fate, a dependence upon chance, and a reliance upon statistical probabilities. Reliance upon these probabilities has taken the place of the Christian doctrine of providence. Conversely, in the face of this secularization I find a large company of friends who can look back on the course of their lives and bear witness to specific times they believed God had delivered them from destruction. They have learned to trust in divine providence.

The central concern of this book has been to contrast the secular faith in luck—good or bad—with the life of faith in the providence of God. Part 1 has been an attempt to lay out the "anatomy of luck." In this discussion, certain ethical issues of great importance were identified: (1) the loneliness of the person whose life is guided aimlessly by fate, chance, the odds, and probabilities stemming from a secular faith in luck; (2) the emptiness and futility of relying on one's own cleverness and skill in manipulating the probabilities of life; (3) the gambler's desire to get money quickly without working; (4) the parasitism of gambling on the body of humanity; (5) the addiction of a significant part of the population to gambling.

Part 2 has offered specific suggestions to pastors and churches to aid them in helping people recognize the difference between luck as a secular faith, on the one hand, and faith in God as the Provider of our basic needs and Deliverer from destruction, on the other hand.

In a crime-ridden, drug-saturated, and self-sufficient populace, dependence upon a faceless, heartless, and unfeeling fate is widespread among us. Turning to the God and Father of our Lord Jesus Christ brings us hope and a new direction for the renewal of our lives. We believe our lives are secure in God's redemptive love in Jesus Christ.

Notes

PREFACE

1. Plato, *Apology,* 38a.
2. See *The Oxford English Dictionary,* vol. 4 (London and New York: Oxford University Press, 1970), 478.

CHAPTER 1. LUCK OR PROVIDENCE?

1. Jonathan Swift, *Gulliver's Travels* (New York: New American Library, 1969), 224, 228–29.
2. William G. Pollard, *Chance and Providence* (New York: Charles Scribner's Sons, 1958), 17.
3. Ibid., 66.
4. Dale Moody, *The Word of Truth* (Grand Rapids: Wm. B. Eerdmans, 1981), 152.
5. Walter Brueggemann, *Power, Providence, and Personality* (Louisville, Ky.: Westminster/John Knox Press, 1990), 15.
6. Ibid., 15, 48.
7. Paul Tillich, *Systematic Theology,* vol. 1 (Chicago: University of Chicago Press, 1951), 267.
8. Leslie Weatherhead, *Salute to a Sufferer* (New York: Abingdon Press, 1962), 40.
9. Roger Shinn, *Forced Options* (New York: Harper & Row, 1982), 224–26.
10. Samuel Taylor Coleridge, *The Rime of the Ancient Mariner,* pt. v.
11. Martin Buber, *Between Man and Man,* trans. Ronald Gregor Smith (London: Routledge & Kegan Paul, 1947), 31.
12. Ernest Payne, *The Fellowship of Believers* (London: Carey Kingsgate Press, 1944), 26.

CHAPTER 2. DRIVING
FORCES OF THE BELIEF IN LUCK

1. Paul Tillich, *Systematic Theology,* vol. 3 (Chicago: University of Chicago Press, 1963), 51.
2. J. Pedersen, *Israel: Its Life and Culture,* vols. 1 and 2 (London: Geoffrey Cumberlege, 1926), 456, 472.
3. William Cowper, "God Moves in a Mysterious Way," *Pilgrim Hymnal:* (Boston: Pilgrim Press, 1958), 88.
4. Lin Yutang, *The Importance of Living* (New York: John Day, 1937), 160.

5. *The Nation,* March 28, 1992, p. 1.

6. Amy Tan, *The Joy Luck Club* (New York: Ballantine Books, 1989), 10–11.

7. Roger Shinn, *Forced Options* (New York: Harper & Row, 1982), 221–22.

8. Gardner Murphy, *Personality: A Biosocial Approach to Origins and Structure* (New York: Harper & Brothers, 1947), 910.

9. Rudolf Otto, *The Idea of the Holy,* trans. John W. Harvey (New York: Oxford University Press, 1923).

10. Ibid., 15, 21, 23.

11. Harry Stack Sullivan, *The Interpersonal Theory of Psychiatry* (New York: W. W. Norton, 1953), 315.

12. Otto, *The Idea of the Holy,* 31.

13. Samuel Southard, *Family Counseling in East Asia* (Manila: New Day Publishers, 1969), 106–7.

CHAPTER 3. FATALISM

1. Plato, *The Republic,* chap. 10, sec. 617–18, in vol. 7 of Great Books of the Western World, *Encyclopaedia Britannica* (Chicago: William Benton, Publisher, 1952), 439.

2. Marcus Aurelius, *Meditations,* bk. 5, sec. 8, in vol. 12 of Great Books of the Western World, 270.

3. Ibid., bk. 5, sec. 19, p. 272.

4. William E. Henley, "Invictus," in *A Treasury of Great Poems,* 2d ed., ed. Louis Untermeyer (New York: Simon & Schuster, 1955), 984.

5. Karen Bloomquist, *The Dream Betrayed: The Religious Challenge of the Working Class* (Minneapolis: Augsburg Fortress, 1990), 31.

6. Marcus Aurelius, *Meditations,* bk. 2, sec. 8, in vol. 12 of Great Books of the Western World, 269.

7. Benedict de Spinoza, *Ethics,* pt. 1, def. 7, in vol. 31 of Great Books of the Western World, 355.

8. Ibid., proposition 27, p. 365.

9. Sir Isaac Newton, *Optics,* bk. 3, pt. 1, in vol. 34 of Great Books of the Western World, 365.

10. Karl Marx, *Das Kapital,* in vol. 50 of Great Books of the Western World, 35, 10, 416.

11. Sigmund Freud, *Origin and Development of Psychoanalysis,* in vol. 48 of Great Books of the Western World, 13.

12. Sigmund Freud, *The Interpretation of Dreams,* in vol. 54 of Great Books of the Western World, 246; idem, *A General Introduction to Psychoanalysis,* in vol. 54 of Great Books of the Western World, 454.

13. See Anthony E. James and Bertram J. Cohler, *The Invulnerable Child* (New York: Haworth Press, 1987).

14. William James, *Principles of Psychology,* vol. 53 of Great Books of the Western World, 823.

15. Ibid., 836.

16. Hans Kohut, *Self Psychology and the Humanities* (New York: W. W. Norton, 1985), 15–16.

17. John Calvin, *The Institutes of the Christian Religion,* vol. 2, bk. 3, chap. 21, trans. Henry Beveridge (Grand Rapids: Wm. B. Eerdmans, 1957), 203.

18. Ludwig von Bertalanffy, *General Systems Theory,* rev. ed. (New York: George Braziller, 1968), 39.

CHAPTER 4. CHANCE

1. Plato, *Timaeus,* sec. 46, in vol. 7 of Great Books of the Western World, *Encyclopaedia Britannica* (Chicago: William Benton, Publisher, 1952), 454.

2. Augustine, *Confessions,* bk. 4, sec. 5, in vol. 18 of Great Books of the Western World, 20.

3. Aristotle, *Physics,* bk. 2, chap. 4, in vol. 8 of Great Books of the Western World, 274.

4. *The Columbia Encyclopedia,* 3d ed. (New York: Columbia University Press, 1963), 929.

5. Aristotle, *Physics,* 274.

6. Colin Brown, *Miracles and the Critical Mind* (Grand Rapids: Wm. B. Eerdmans, 1984), 174.

7. William G. Pollard, *Chance and Providence* (New York: Charles Scribner's Sons, 1958), 94.

8. Rollo May, *The Meaning of Anxiety* (New York: Ronald Press, 1950), 3.

9. Archibald MacLeish, *J.B.* (Boston: Houghton Mifflin, 1958), 47.

10. Robert Hendrickson, *The Facts on File Encyclopedia of Word and Phrase Origins* (New York: Facts on File Publications, 1987), 77.

11. *The Poems of Robert Frost* (New York: Modern Library, 1930), 41.

12. An esteemed colleague, Professor Samuel Southard, and I collaborated on the following discussion of illusions. The discussion was very enlightening to me, and I am in his debt for much of this. He is Senior Research Professor at Southern Baptist Theological Seminary and Professor of Pastoral Theology Emeritus, Fuller Theological Seminary.

13. Erich Fromm, *Ye Shall Be as Gods* (New York: Holt, Rinehart & Winston, 1966), 23.

14. Rollo May, *The Art of Counseling,* rev. ed. (New York: Gardner Press, 1989), 142–43.

15. See Søren Kierkegaard, *The Sickness unto Death* (Princeton: Princeton University Press, 1951), 44–53, esp. p. 44.

16. Ibid., 63.

17. Ibid., 69.

18. Roy Grinker, M.D., and John Spiegel, *Men Under Stress* (New York: Blakiston, 1945), 157, 361, 363.

CHAPTER 5. PROBABILITY

1. Carl Sifakis, *The Encyclopedia of Gambling* (New York: Facts on File, 1990), 128.

2. *Encyclopaedia Britannica,* 15th ed., s.v. "probability."

3. Adapted from information appearing in the *New England Journal of Medi-*

cine, Robert D. Trugg, Allen S. Brett, and Joel Frader, "The Problem with Futility," vol. 328, no. 23, pp. 1560–64, June 4, 1992. Used by permission.
    4. *Mayo Clinic Health Letter,* February 1992.
    5. Adapted from information appearing in the *New England Journal of Medicine,* David Hilfiker, M.D., "Facing Our Mistakes," vol. 310, no. 2, pp. 118–22, January 12, 1984. Used by permission.
    6. *(Louisville) Courier Journal,* July 1, 1992.
    7. *Christian Science Monitor,* June 25, 1992.
    8. *The Histories of Herodotus,* trans. H. Carter (New York: Heritage Press, 1958). Reported by Richard S. Broughton, *Parapsychology: The Controversial Science* (New York: Ballantine Press, 1991), 50–51.
    9. The information in this section on parapsychology comes from Broughton, *Parapsychology.*

CHAPTER 6. GAMBLING

    1. This material on the history of gambling is abstracted from *Encyclopaedia Britannica,* 17th ed., s.v., "gambling."
    2. See my book *When Religion Gets Sick* (Philadelphia: Westminster Press, 1969).
    3. Carl Sifakis, *The Encyclopedia of Gambling* (New York: Facts on File, 1990), 32.
    4. Fyodor Dostoyevsky, *The Gambler* (London: Penguin Books, 1966), 14.
    5. Ibid., 40.
    6. Ibid., 44, 45.
    7. Ibid., 93.
    8. Ibid., 161–62.
    9. Edmund Bergler, *The Psychology of Gambling* (1958; reprint, New York: International Universities Press, 1970), 7.
    10. Dostoyevsky, *The Gambler,* 129.
    11. Bergler, *The Psychology of Gambling,* 9.
    12. Ibid., 19.
    13. Ibid., 20.
    14. *Diagnostic and Statistical Manual of Mental Disorders,* 3d ed. (Washington, D.C.: American Psychiatric Association, 1987), 325.
    15. Bergler, *The Psychology of Gambling,* 129.
    16. Gerald G. May, *Addiction and Grace* (New York: Harper & Row, 1988), 155–61.
    17. Bergler, *The Psychology of Gambling,* 56.
    18. Sifakis, *The Encyclopedia of Gambling,* 182.
    19. Ibid., 183.
    20. Ibid., 7.
    21. Ibid., 187.
    22. Ibid., 189.
    23. Ibid.

CHAPTER 7. PASTORAL RESPONSES
TO SECULAR FAITH IN LUCK

1. *(Louisville) Courier Journal,* October 1 and 2, 1993.

2. Scott Peck, *The People of the Lie* (New York: Simon & Schuster, 1993), 37–84.

3. See Fyodor Dostoyevsky, *The Gambler* (London: Penguin Books, 1966); also see chap. 6.

4. Wayne E. Oates, *Temptation: A Biblical and Psychological Perspective* (Louisville, Ky.: Westminster/John Knox Press, 1991).

5. Gerald May, *Addiction and Grace* (New York: Harper & Row, 1988), 139.

6. "Prospice," in *The Poems and Plays of Robert Browning,* ed. Saxe Commins (New York: Modern Library, 1954), 318.

7. Eric Berne, *Transactional Analysis in Psychotherapy* (New York: Grove Press, 1981), 112.

CHAPTER 8. CONGREGATIONAL RESPONSES
TO SECULAR FAITH IN LUCK

1. "Responsible Fatherhood," *Christian Science Monitor,* December 6, 1993.

2. "Gambling's Illusion," *Christian Science Monitor,* January 19, 1994.

3. *The Serious Sides of Sex,* ed. Neville Blakemore and Neville Blakemore, Jr. (Louisville, Ky.: Nevbet Company, 1991).

4. "Gambling," *Mayo Clinic Health Letter,* November 1993.

5. *Diagnostic and Statistical Manual of Mental Disorders,* 3d ed. (Washington, D.C.: American Psychiatric Association, 1987), 325.

6. "Gambling's False Promise," *Christian Science Monitor,* November 15, 1993.